Praise for Floyd Skloot's memoir, *A World of Light*

"This collection of brilliant essays bears witness to the astonishing strength, spirit, and sense of humor with which [Skloot] has reconstructed his life and personal history."—*Booklist* (starred review)

"The book is more than a collection of the personal memories he so doggedly seeks; it also functions as a reflection about cognition, literature and writing, music, growing up and simple living. The author's immense effort in putting back together his mental and physical life is at turns funny, chilling and inspiring. He goes beyond merely making sense of his condition by showing how reaching outward can heal one's inner damage."—*Publishers Weekly*

"[An] accomplished essayist excavates his past, including a bout of lost memory and his mother's Alzheimer's."—Editors' Choice, *New York Times Book Review*

"Simultaneously humorous, frightening, and sad, the essays capture the world in which increasingly more elderly people live, where the body has outlived the mind. . . . These human and engaging familial essays make us realize the necessity of living fully in the present."—*Library Journal*

"[Skloot] offers spare sentences that evoke a world. . . . Deserves a wide audience."—*Kirkus Reviews*

"The author is a talented writer for whom literary creativity is clearly an essential part of how he navigates life with his own memory impairment. . . . The book is recommended for medical humanities courses, especially those for which writings on the experience of neurologic devastation would be worthwhile. The essays are well written and at times quite amusing, despite the seriousness of the topic."—*Journal of the American Medical Association*

"A masterful effort. Words like 'nourishing' and 'grace' paint a fair picture of reviewers' tones; they respect his accomplishment as much as they respect the effort that must have gone into creating it. It makes one believe that, if we only remembered what was important, life might be much more rewarding."—*Bookmarks Magazine* (four stars)

"Breathtaking. . . . Skloot writes with eloquence and humor. . . . Skloot's memoir is constructed much the way his memories now work, moving back and forth through time, zipping from one subject to the next, and all the while creating indelible portraits of Skloot's life with both his mother and his supportive wife. Buttressing the story are fascinating details about how and what we remember, why emotionally tinged memories stay more powerfully in our mind, and how Skloot's writing keeps the virus that seems hellbent on quieting him at bay. 'The thing I had to do was write about the experience, refuse the silence,' Skloot says. And here, he's done it brilliantly and with grace."—Caroline Leavitt, *Boston Globe*

"The emotion here runs deep, but it is contained by the author's probing intelligence. . . . Skloot knows something of grace, but he has left failure far behind. He has painstakingly rebuilt his life and his art, shaping the experience of crippling illness into dazzling literature. . . . Floyd Skloot is the Willie Mays of memoirists."—Mark Essig, *San Francisco Chronicle*

"Each of his chapters can be read as an essay. The book as a whole, however, paints a picture of a son's renascence and mother's demise, of transitions that are complex at best and made more difficult by diseases that are horrific in their courses and consequences."—*Chicago Tribune*

Praise for Floyd Skloot's memoir, *In the Shadow of Memory*

In this remarkable collection of essays, part of the American Lives series (edited by Tobias Wolff), Skloot conveys what it is like to live with a damaged brain. . . . This is an unusual and engrossing memoir written with intelligence, honesty, perception and humor."—*Publishers Weekly*

"Skloot has created a luminous yet brutally candid memoir. . . . This book possesses a gravity and immensity that belie its brief length."—Julia Keller, *Chicago Tribune*

"Bracingly triumphant. . . . [Skloot] is a master of the genre, deftly incorporating neuroscience and autobiography, vivid detail and hard-won emotional truth. . . . Think of *In the Shadow of Memory* as an Oliver Sacks work written from the inside out, the neurological patient as narrator of his own condition."—Dan Cryer, *Newsday*

"Tightly written and beautifully constructed. . . . A tribute to the creative spirit, which is beyond anything as fragile as the thinking mind."—David Guy, *Seattle Times*

"The mind that created these pages may be halting, but it is entirely whole. . . . These chapters of family memory are tightly written and beautifully constructed, so we are astonished toward the end of one when Skloot mentions that it has taken him 11 months to write 13 pages. Earlier he had spoken of writing as a way of facing down the 'insult' of his injury. This whole book is an instance of that, and a tribute to the creative spirit, which is beyond anything as fragile as the thinking mind."—David Guy, *Washington Post*

"Never self-indulgent, the book is a clear-eyed investigation into our powers of recall, especially as they relate to painful familial pasts, and a look at how we never stop trying to make something transcendent of our disturbing memories. . . . With this searing honesty, Skloot's essays add up to a profoundly moving tale of emotion triumphing over the analytical, of the importance of accepting family shortcomings rather than trying to rewrite the past. The world Skloot delineates is one in which brain damage, like troubled family histories, offers backhanded kinds of blessings—blessings he nonetheless celebrates with refreshing candor."—Bernadette Murphy, *Los Angeles Times*

"What will amaze readers . . . is the poise—and even humor—with which Skloot turns personal catastrophe into literary reflection. These reflections convert neurological fact into poignant insight on how brain failure at once imperils and reveals the human essence. . . . Perhaps because so many of his memories have vanished into the black hole of disease, Skloot unfolds each of his remaining recollections as fragments of a precious mosaic of meaning. A remarkable literary achievement."—*Booklist*

The Wink of the Zenith

The Wink *of the* Zenith

The Shaping of a Writer's Life

Floyd Skloot

UNIVERSITY OF NEBRASKA PRESS—LINCOLN & LONDON

Acknowledgments for the use of
previously published material
appear on pages xiii–xiv,
which constitute an extension
of the copyright page.

∞

Library of Congress Cataloging-
in-Publication Data
Skloot, Floyd.
The wink of the zenith:
the shaping of a writer's life
/ Floyd Skloot.
p. cm.
ISBN 978-0-8032-1119-3
(cloth: alk. paper)
1. Skloot, Floyd—Childhood and
youth. 2. Authors, American—20th
century—Biography. I. Title.
PS3569.K577Z46 2008
818'.54—dc22 [B]

2008003674

For Beverly

It is our inward journey that leads us
through time—forward or back,
seldom in a straight line, most often spiraling.
Each of us is moving, changing with
respect to others. As we discover, we remember;
remembering, we discover.

—Eudora Welty, *One Writer's Beginnings*

Contents

Preface

In December of 1988, when I was forty-one, I contracted a virus that targeted my brain and left me in neurological tatters. I couldn't write, and struggled to understand the simplest sentences I read. My memory systems were wrecked, leaving me unable to store new information or reliably find and assemble old information. I had difficulty learning things and was easily lost. My word-finding and concentration powers were compromised, abstract reasoning and the capacity to form structures were damaged, IQ diminished nearly twenty percent. I walked with a cane for the next fifteen years.

At the time I got sick, I'd been publishing poetry for twenty years, short stories for fifteen years, and had completed the manuscripts of two novels and most of a third that would all appear in the 1990s. My poems were generally short, lyric pieces, tightly structured. My fiction, also tightly structured, emerged from characters and their voices, with minimal plots (and minimal readership). I'd never written personal essays or memoir. My only nonfiction writing was book reviews and memos or position papers in my work as staff to various governors or legislators or corporate management.

Illness silenced me for a year. What returned first were scattered images and phrases I would jot down in bedside notebooks quickly, before they vanished from short-term memory. Soon I had pads and index cards and post-it notes everywhere, because I could never risk waiting till I could locate one. It was two years before I tried to write anything more sustained than a short poem, before I could begin to piece together the notes jotted down here and there, and find something like coherence among them.

I needed to write about what was happening to me, but realized that poetry, as I was capable of writing it, wouldn't allow the scale of exploration I was after. Without the capacity to make structure or develop abstract thoughts, working in snippets of a few minutes at a time, proceeding with little idea of where I was heading, I had to come up with a new way to write at length. And to my genuine surprise, the genre I turned to was memoir.

The impulse to write fiction had vanished along with the voices that used to trigger it. The lesions on my brain, holes scattered throughout the cerebral cortex, were where I believed those voices had gone. In their place, it seemed, was my own voice, distant still but demanding that I tell my own story. By writing about it, I began to combat an illness that seemed determined to silence me.

In a way that sounds melodramatic but is true, the memoir, in its flexibility and formal openness, saved me as a writer. It allowed me to give full voice to my experience, fragment by fragment. The process enabled me to put shards of memory back together, create some sort of window into my past, so I could see who I was and connect him with the person I had become.

Fiction was not an option, but even if it were, I don't believe fiction would have worked for me. I needed to tell the truth, without making anything up, because it was the only way I could understand what I was going through. I needed to find out how the pieces I'd jotted down fit together, work I could only do by writing, by putting them on the page, seeing what I had, and discovering where it led. Thinking, with my limitations, would not work.

The Wink of the Zenith is the fourth memoir I've written in the twenty years since getting sick. But it's the first that isn't about being sick, or reassembling myself in the aftermath of a neurological calamity, or finding my way back into the world as a disabled man. It's about the shaping of a writer's life, about the forces that made me the sort of person who could only deal with what happened to him by writing about it.

The book's first half concerns external influences within the family, close friendships, community, popular culture, or experiences which bear upon the formation of character, sensibility, and habits of mind. The second half concerns how that sensibility gives shape to the life being lived, making sense of the random, often disconnected facts of experience.

I didn't know what *The Wink of the Zenith* would be when I started writing it. As with all the work I've written in the last two decades, there was no plan or outline, no governing concept, only the gradual discovery of how pieces fit together. In the wake of brain damage, I'm simply not capable of the sort of thought or organization, the conceptualization, that would be required for such an approach. To theorize about how I became a writer, and how writing shapes my life now, requires levels of abstraction and reasoning that are beyond my abilities. But by making brief notes, capturing shards of memory or thought, writing out specific scenes, I began to discover what they meant and how they might cohere. So this book enacts the process it describes, the shaping of a writing life.

Acknowledgments

Chapters of *The Wink of the Zenith* originally appeared in the following publications, sometimes in different versions, and I thank the editors for their support of my work:

Boulevard: "Jambon Dreams" and "The Summer of the Vampire."

Colorado Review: "Echo Lark," "Numbers," and "The Voice of the Past."

Creative Nonfiction: "Going, Going, Gone."

Los Angeles Review: "Home Economics for Halfbacks."

New Letters: "Travels in Lavender and Light."

Ninth Letter: "Bewitched, Bothered and Bewildered."

Northwest Review: "Flesh and Fortune: Coming Back to *Measure for Measure*."

Oregon Literary Review: reprinted "The Summer of the Vampire."

The Pinch: "Silence the Pianos."

Prairie Schooner: "Cover Stories."

River Teeth: "Shine On."

The Sewanee Review: "Into a Maelstrom of Fire: On Having a Feeling for Thomas Hardy."

Southwest Review: "The Wink of the Zenith."

Virginia Quarterly Review: "When the Clock Stops" and part of the preface under the title "Turning to Memoir."

Witness: Childhood in America: "Running After My Father."

The final section of "Bewitched, Bothered and Bewildered" was published by the *New York Times Magazine* under the title "Are You My Mother?"

"The Voice of the Past" won a Pushcart Prize and will be included in *Pushcart Prize XXXIII*, 2009.

"Jambon Dreams" was reprinted in *Best Food Writing 2006*, edited by Holly Hughes (Marlowe and Company, 2006) and was cited for Special Mention in *Pushcart Prize XXXII*, 2008.

"Cover Stories" was cited as a Notable Essay of 2006 in *The Best American Essays 2007* and received a Glenna Luschei *Prairie Schooner* Award for 2006.

"Going, Going, Gone" was selected for Notable Sports Writing of 2005 in *The Best American Sports Writing 2006*.

"Running After My Father" was cited for Special Mention in *Pushcart Prize XXXI*, 2007.

"Into a Maelstrom of Fire: On Having a Feeling for Thomas Hardy" and "When the Clock Stops" are dedicated to Robert Russell, my earliest mentor.

I thank The Rockefeller Foundation for a residency at their Study and Conference Center in Bellagio, Italy, during the time this book was begun. My agent, Andrew Blauner, was again generous with his time and steady in his friendship. My editor, Ladette Randolph, has graciously supported and strengthened my work through three books now. My daughter, Rebecca Skloot, gave time, attention, and advice though working under deadlines to complete her own articles and book. My wife, Beverly Hallberg, is this book's guiding force with her love, insight, faith, and honesty.

The Wink of the Zenith

Part One

Home Economics for Halfbacks

Childhood is the seedbed of all later
understanding and expression.

—Sven Birkerts, *My Sky Blue Trades*

I

Going, Going, Gone

I was standing in the bedroom of our Brooklyn apartment with my ear pressed to the radio. It was dark outside, a spring evening in the mid-1950s, and through the open window I could hear people talking in the courtyard four stories below. I was eight or nine years old, and my brother Philip, a teenager, was sitting at his desk bent over homework. That explains why the radio's volume was turned so low. Philip couldn't hear it over the courtyard chatter or else he'd have told me to turn it down.

I'd succeeded in losing myself to the world of baseball, and could hardly stand still as I leaned farther into the radio. If you could see me shuffling in place, cheek-to-cheek with a console the same size that I am, arms gripping its sides, you might think we were dancing.

My father had taken me to many games at Ebbets Field, a few at the Polo Grounds, even one at Yankee Stadium. I'd collected baseball cards since I was six, played punchball and stickball and baseball for hours in the spring and summer, invented games to play by myself with baseball cards on the apartment floor, read baseball magazines and books, studied batting statistics. So I knew what I was listening to. I also knew what I was waiting for.

If it was a Yankees game on the radio, I was waiting for Mel Allen to call out "Going, going, gone" when a home run was hit. If it was a Giants game, I was hoping Russ Hodges would scream "Bye bye baby." And if it was a Dodgers game, which is most likely, I wanted Vin Scully's curt "Gone!" I was homer-happy. But it was the announcer's call, not the hit itself, that captivated me.

When it came, when the batter's sudden triumph was described in language so potent with loss, I was never able to keep silent. *Going, going, gone.* To realize such success required bidding adieu to what made it possible, *Bye bye baby,* and the delight in the announcer's voice counterpointed with his actual words packed an emotional wallop I found overwhelming. The ball was *Gone!* for good and so was my last vestige of composure.

Philip would get up, cross the room, turn the radio off, and stalk back to his desk. He may even have socked me on the shoulder. But I'd have had what I wanted: a moment when arrival and departure were poised, when the offense's joyful achievement was mingled with the defense's sad failure in phrases and tones that acknowledged the whole knotted experience.

My connection with these Dodgers of the 1950s felt deeply personal. The players and their families lived in Brooklyn, could be seen on the streets, on the subway. They were known to us by intimate names, Campy and Robby, Junior and Shotgun, Duke and Rube. When my brother at age seven was hospitalized because shards of glass had slashed his right eye, the Dodgers' shortstop and captain, Pee Wee Reese, came to visit him. Pee Wee sat on Philip's hospital bed and gave him an autographed baseball. Also two tickets to a double-header in early September, as incentive for steady healing. Why, Pee Wee was practically family! So was Gil Hodges, since I had a Hodges-model baseball glove, a big trapper's mitt used only by first basemen. Because I was so small, the one position I'd never play was first base, but I admired Hodges for his calm, quiet ways, his steady power, the etched glower with which he stared at an opposing pitcher. I wanted to be like him, and when I wore the glove that bore his name, I almost was. Then, when the young pitching star, Karl Spooner, hurt his arm and was unable to play again, I placed his baseball card on my desk in tribute, and surrounded it with clippings from the newspaper like a shrine for a lost relative. Soon enough, a twinge developed in my own arm from the torque of imaginary curve balls. Carl Furillo in right field was nicknamed Skoonj, for his love of conch: *scungili*. Skoonj sounded a bit like Skloot, so I imagined that we were related too. Somewhere back in the old country, I decided, his family and mine had once lived in the same village, somewhere near the sea, where we all developed our passion for shellfish. Then his family moved to Italy and mine moved to Russia, their names got rearranged, and we didn't come together again till we both ended up in Brooklyn. That explained it.

Living in Brooklyn and rooting for the Dodgers felt so natural that it was unquestioned, like my affinity for raw clams (!) from Sheepshead Bay, or chicken from my father's poultry market. But then came October 1957. The publicist for Brooklyn Dodgers announced on October eighth that the team was moving to Los Angeles. They'd played their last game in Brooklyn the month before; the Brooklyn Dodgers were no more. And the next week the Skloot family was moving too, leaving Brooklyn on October fifteenth. I always felt the two moves were connected, regardless of what my parents said.

I remember two formal farewells to Brooklyn. I was ten, and we were going to live in Long Beach, off the south shore of Long Island, and nothing I could say would change that. My parents' key promotional points—that we'd be renting the top half of a private home instead of living in an apartment, that we'd be living just a few hundred yards from the ocean, that I'd have all new friends and new places to play with them—meant nothing to me. I knew my way around our Brooklyn block. I had friends in the apartment building and at school, and could find places to go when my parents raged. But Long

Beach and its ocean were like the surface of Venus to me, covered in dense clouds, unknowable, alien. I had a map of the heavens on my bedroom wall and already knew all I cared to know about hostile environments. I didn't like visiting Long Beach when we were looking for our new home, and couldn't imagine adapting to life there. It just did not make any sense to me, which is why I never believed the official family explanations.

Nonetheless, we were moving on Tuesday. My father had sold his kosher poultry market and agreed to begin working for my mother's brother, managing a dress-making factory; my mother had been looking for new furniture with my aunt, who was an interior decorator; my brother had graduated from high school and was attending New York University, complaining about how much worse his commute would be when we moved; my toys and clothes and books were packed in cartons, everything except my baseball card collection, which would travel to Long Beach with me in the car, like my mother's jewelry and my father's cigars.

The first formal farewell occurred just before school let out on Monday. My fifth grade teacher asked me to stand and face the class so everyone could say "Good-bye, Floyd," in unison, as though pledging allegiance to the flag. Except they broke into laughter afterward.

Then I was in the fenced playground outside the school building, standing where home plate was marked in fading white paint, and my friends were spread out in their usual positions for our daily punchball game. I bounced the red rubber ball five times, as always, threw it a few inches in the air, and punched it over the left fielder's head. As I ran, I decided to keep going till I scored or was tagged out. All-or-nothing now in my final turn as a Brooklyn punchball star. I wish memory's highlight reel ended there, with my ten-year-old self flying around the schoolyard bases in a last mad dash toward home. But I remember the play simply coming to a halt as I stopped dead, halfway between second base and third, sobbing, gasping for breath. I sat abruptly on the asphalt, shocked, unable to control my crying. Everyone gathered around me as though I were hurt, giving me room but watching until an older boy who lived in my apartment building stepped forward to help me up and walk me home.

The day we moved, I had the Asian flu. My fever began Monday night and by Tuesday was 103 degrees. As I lay in bed that night in a room that no longer looked like my own, with everything packed away and the walls bare except for a few errant strips of dark scotch tape, I kept remembering myself a few hours earlier on the school-yard, collapsed in tears between bases. Who was that person? Had the event really happened, or was it all a fever dream? If it had happened, maybe the flu had caused it. My imagination and memory consorted in that now-strange bed to form something new, something surreal and never to be lost, an image of myself as I could not imagine myself being.

I wasn't able to go to school for the first week we lived in Long Beach. But one afternoon when the fever was almost gone, my teacher came to visit us at home. This was something new, too, a teacher in my home, in my room, and I wasn't sure I liked it. The visit confirmed what I already knew: Long Beach was going to be a strange place. To make matters even odder, my teacher was a man. Mr. Lee was tall and heavy and Chinese, and my whole world seemed to be re-forming as a fever dream. He brought me a couple of schoolbooks and sat on my desk chair. He even picked up my stack of last year's baseball cards, removed the rubber band, and flipped through them. I could see that nothing was sacred around here.

By the time he'd come to visit, my room was set up the way I wanted it. I'd surrounded myself with baseball cards, back issues of *Sport* magazine, and my dice baseball game paraphernalia, which included a thick notebook of statistics for every player on every team. He touched it all. He leafed through the notebook, then looked over at me. I could tell that he thought I was strange too.

"So," Mr. Lee said, "you like baseball?" When I nodded, he added, "maybe you can give us a report on it in class."

That sounded exceptional. So I modestly informed him of my related scholastic interests: "I'm pretty good at punchball and stickball too. And football. I could give a report on that also."

"Tackle or touch?"

This was very promising. A teacher who could talk about sports, who came to your house to welcome you, who knew how to handle baseball cards and talk at the same time. Even knew the right terms to use when talking about football. Maybe I could forgive him for handling my things.

On my first day as a fifth grader in Mr. Lee's class, I got into a fight with Big Eli Haas during recess. He kept calling me "new kid" and pushing me when I went to field a ball, which made me lose my balance and miss the catch. People would think I was a lousy fielder, something I couldn't bear, so I finally turned on Eli and tackled him. In a flash, Mr. Lee had picked me up by the belt and lifted me away. It was as though he knew something like this was going to happen, and had been watching out for it.

My punishment for fighting was extra homework: I had to write that composition about baseball. Punishment as reward! When he saw me smile, Mr. Lee made sure I understood that my other homework had to be done first.

On the school bus going home, I tried to decide who or what I'd write about. My favorite player? I didn't want to offend Pee Wee Reese by writing about Gil Hodges, or vice versa, even though Hodges had been an All-Star in 1957. Jackie Robinson was retired. Roy Campanella was getting old and had just endured a poor season, something I didn't want to mention to anyone in case they didn't already know about it. There were the other Dodgers All-Stars, Gino Cimoli and Clem

Labine, one new to the team, the other an old-timer already, players with curious names, almost as memorable as George Shuba's. And there were the young pitchers, Don Drysdale and Sandy Koufax, but I hadn't yet decided between them, even though Koufax was Jewish and therefore also part of my family. No, clearly I would have to write about something other than my favorite player.

When it occurred to me that I should write about the Dodgers moving to Los Angeles, I almost had my second public crying fit of the month. I didn't know if I could manage it, wondered if I should wait until I didn't feel so unhappy about the subject. Nah, better to face the truth.

After I finished my other homework and ate dinner, I sat at my desk and tried to write. My family thought I was playing dice baseball, as usual, and left me alone, but I couldn't even begin my assignment. The problem was how to get past the phrase "The Los Angeles Dodgers" in the first sentence. So I wrote about my baseball card collection instead of the Dodgers' relocation, explaining in great detail how hard it was for me to find a 1957 Ed Roebuck card to complete my set, because I'd lost mine during our move, the season was over, and 1957 cards were no longer for sale. I think I was hoping Mr. Lee, who clearly admired my collection when he'd visited, might have an Ed Roebuck card of his own and be moved to give it to me.

There was a tall, thick oak tree across the street from our house in Long Beach. Its trunk was the ideal width to represent a strike zone when I played wiffle ball with my neighbor, Jay Shaffer.

One of us stood by the wiffle ball tree, bat cocked, while the other stood across Coolidge Avenue at the top of my slanted driveway, ball in hand, ready to pitch. If the batter didn't swing and the pitch hit the tree, it was a strike. If it missed the tree, it was a ball and the batter had to go chase it down the street.

Pitching well with a wiffle ball required craft and dedication. The hollow plastic ball, with its pattern of eight oblong cutouts, could be made to curve and dip, to rise, to dart toward or away from a batter. But it was difficult to control the movement. The art of wiffle ball pitching revealed itself as I realized that the slower I threw a ball, the more it moved. Gripping adjacent holes with thumb and index finger, twisting my wrist as I threw, I could make the ball swoop and plunge like a crazed hawk. I worked hard to master a pitch that reversed directions in midair, practicing for hours against the garage door, each pitch leaving a small smudge on the white paint.

After 1958, I was always aware that behind the garage door, resting against the far wall, was a box containing torn and bloody clothes belonging to my father. He'd been wearing them as he stood behind his Buick, about to open the trunk and change a flat tire. A green Ford careened off the road and smashed into him, pinning his body between the two cars and crushing his legs.

The box, I'd been told, contained evidence for a trial that would occur some day. I was not to open it because the air or my fingerprints would ruin the evidence. But I knew I was not to open it because it would be horrible to see what was inside, which meant that I couldn't stop imagining it.

I opened the box in November 1959, when I was twelve and alone because my mother was visiting my father in the hospital. My father's trousers were on top, a black heap crusty with dried blood, and I didn't touch them. Couldn't touch them. Poking out beneath were the toes of his brown wing-tip shoes, striated with more dried blood, the tails of his white dress shirt looking as though they had been dipped in blood as well, and his dark stiffened socks scrunched against the side of the box. The only item in the box that I picked up was an envelope which had been stuffed beside the socks. Inside, I found three black and white photographs of my father lying on the ground behind his crumpled white Buick. He was on his back, glasses gone, forearms raised as though warding off more blows. I wondered who had taken these photographs. A passerby? A journalist? The driver of the other car?

Every time I threw the wiffle ball at the garage, I felt as though I were throwing it at that man who'd injured my father. I knew his name was Mr. Pincus and that he owned a delicatessen at the west end of town. The garage door handle was Mr. Pincus's heart. In time, I could make the crazed hawk attack that heart at will.

My father spent most of the two years after his accident in hospitals. First, he was in a ward at Queens General Hospital, near the site of the crash, as his massive injuries healed. Then he came home for a month, sleeping in a rented hospital bed, before entering Long Beach Hospital for surgery to re-break his legs, which had healed wrong. A child, I wasn't allowed to visit him. When he finally returned home, in early 1960, his hair had turned gray, his skin sagged from his face, he smelled strange, and he couldn't get out of bed. It took another half year for him to be mobile enough, using a wheelchair and then canes, to return to work in the dress factory.

Every Monday morning, he would be driven into New York by my brother, who was also working in New York City, selling adhesive-backed papers. They would stay together in a midtown hotel during the week and return home on Friday evening.

I would always contrive to be outside, playing with Jay or by myself, waiting for their car to arrive. Jay and I, using the inflexible arrangement of house, tree, street, and sidewalk, had designed a wiffle ball "stadium" that included my front porch, jutting into the playing field like short bleachers in left field. It made sense to us because the real Dodgers were now playing in a Los Angeles stadium that contained left field bleachers only a short distance from home plate. We decreed that any batted ball landing on the porch and managing not to roll off under the railing was a home run. So was a ball hit onto the house's roof. If it struck the house above the garage but below the living room window, it was a double; above the window, it was a triple. A ball the pitcher couldn't catch was a single; anything the pitcher caught was an out.

In early November 1961, as we played an important contest between the Dodgers and Giants in the dwindling light before dinner, my father and brother arrived home. The car's horn sounding when they turned onto Coolidge Avenue signaled the impending end of our game. Jay and I waited till the car was parked, then began one final play, which my father as usual watched from the porch.

It was the last time I remember seeing him alive. He stood in the bleachers, one hand gripping the rail, his canes perched against the wall of our house, his other hand moving toward his face for another puff of cigar. He smiled down at me. When I socked a pitch over the roof above him, he waved and called out congratulations: "Atta boy!"

He and my mother left later that evening, in the dark, for a Veterans Day holiday at a resort upstate. He died there, in the swimming pool, at the age of fifty-three. When I recall the telephone ringing to bring us the news, the scene flashes back two days. I have just stroked Jay's fastball—a straight and easy pitch to hit, a gift from my best friend—onto the roof and turned my head to find my father haloed in smoke, laughing now, saying "Atta boy!"

My brother woke up early on the morning of his wedding. We lived in an apartment house again, having moved to a smaller and less expensive place after our father's death. My brother was twenty-four, I was sixteen, and we still shared a room. So I woke up early too. He lit a Kent and told me to get dressed.

It was June 21, 1964, the last day Philip and I would live together. It was also Father's Day, for the last three years a day of sadness to us. Also a day of confusion, since Philip now sometimes acted like a brother, sometimes like a father, and our relationship had taken on a new tension.

Through the apartment's open window, we could hear seagulls bugle above the breakers. The sound always seemed comical to me, a scavenger's cackle, but that morning I heard it as plaintive, almost forlorn. I couldn't sort out my feelings. For two or three years, I'd been looking forward to this day, but dreading it too. Finally, a room of my own! An end to Philip's constant cigarette smoke and pre-dawn coughing spells, access to all the Velveeta in the refrigerator, freedom to sleep or wake when I chose. An end to his teasing about my obsessions with dice baseball and rock 'n' roll, our combat over the tidy way I kept my half of the room, his efforts to sidetrack my homework. But I knew I'd miss him. His sudden generosities, his advice, his willingness to play with me. We wouldn't be watching quiz shows together on the small television beside his bed, trying to be the first with an answer; we wouldn't play games of Careers on his bed or go out for Saturday lunch at Nathan's and see who could eat an ice cream cone faster despite the headache it induced. We wouldn't play touch football anymore with my friends in autumn or softball in summer.

The two of us together could keep our widowed mother at bay. I wasn't sure I could do that solo. Since our father's death, she had been even more volatile than ever, charging at us as we sat in the living room, slapping at our faces for imagined infractions and indignities.

In the last year, she had begun dating. She had also begun working as a travel agent and taking advantage of complimentary travel opportunities, especially cruises, trying to meet her next husband. It was a time of changes in our family, but even at sixteen, when I woke up that first day of summer in 1964, I knew my life was about to be transformed beyond anything that had happened so far.

Philip threw a tee shirt and jeans onto my bed. "Move it, kiddo. We're going to play stickball."

I'd guessed that was what he'd want to do on his wedding day. So I was prepared for him. Stickball was something we'd grown up with on the streets of Brooklyn. We'd played in the apartment's courtyard, on the schoolyard, against any wall we could find. Some of my earliest memories of life with my brother are memories of facing him as he wound up to throw a pitch, or of watching as he swung at a pitch of mine.

In the mind of most kids growing up in 1950s New York, stickball was associated with Willie Mays. The Say Hey Kid! Mays played baseball with sheer joy, and his array of all-around skills seemed unmatched by any other player. We all knew that Mays loved the sport so much he was willing to hang around after a Giants game and play stickball with the kids in upper Harlem. According to George Plimpton, in his essay "Did Willie Hit It for Five Sewers?" there's a legend that Mays had hit a red rubber Spaldeen ball eight hundred feet on the fly, playing in the street rather than against a wall.

Stickball was freedom. It was improvisation. We could play the game anywhere, and we could use almost anything as equipment: a baseball bat, a sawed-off broomstick, or a mop handle, and an official Spaldeen or an old tennis ball with the fuzz worn away. Stickball could be played with just the two of us, or we could team up against other duos.

My brother's brand of stickball combined raw batting power, pitching finesse, a pool shark's sense of angles, and psychological acumen. In the street or on the schoolyard court with a stick or ball in hand, everything came together for him. Cigarette between his lips, right eye half-closed as smoke rose in front of it, he could hit or pitch with grace. Sometimes, if I was at bat first and hadn't yet had a chance to pitch to him, Philip would set the tone for our game by hitting me with his first pitch. Thrown hard enough, a rubber ball stings and leaves behind a circular welt like a stain. Then he would hit me with the second pitch too. And the third. In theory, this put him in a jam because now the bases were loaded, with no outs. But in practice, he didn't worry about baserunners, figuring he could score against me at will. His fourth pitch would hit me as well, granting me a 1–0 lead.

So as we drove from our apartment to the schoolyard, I knew what to expect at the start. But Philip didn't know I'd been working on a hard curve, throwing against the wall of our building in the late afternoons to perfect the pitch before he got home from work. I thought I could begin the bottom half of the first inning by throwing one right at his head, and laughing as he backed away from a pitch that broke into the strike zone.

That was the plan. A going-away surprise from his baby brother, just to say, *don't worry, I'll be okay.*

There was a brief home movie commemorating this June twenty-first game. I can't remember who took the film, but the view was from over my shoulder as I stared at Philip in the distance. If I watched the film closely enough, I could see the cigarette in my brother's mouth moving up and down: he was talking to me, razzing me as I wound up to pitch. Then he uncoiled and walloped whatever it was that I offered him, not fazed by my fast ball or new curve, and the final image showed him leaning back against the wall for balance, head up, laughing as he watched the ball vanish in the distance.

I remember a recurring dream in which I played center field for the Brooklyn Dodgers, wearing my white-and-blue pinstriped pajamas as a uniform, and was able to run the bases or chase after long fly balls without my feet touching the ground. I was so fast that I flew, though the dream never included my scoring a run or catching a ball.

To adults who asked me what I wanted to be when I grew up, as a child I automatically said *center fielder for the Dodgers,* believing that it was important to specify a position if my intentions were to be taken seriously. I kept saying *center fielder for the Dodgers* even after the franchise moved from Brooklyn, though I no longer rooted for them, and even after I began to play second base for my high school's freshman team instead of center field.

Sometime around the age of fifteen, I believe I knew, deep down, that I wasn't going to be a professional baseball player. The "growth spurt," long predicted by my mother and doctor, deserted me at five feet four inches and only confirmed what I'd already understood: I was too small. Besides, in the rare moments of honesty about my baseball talent, I could admit that I wasn't good enough. In all my years playing baseball, or slow-pitch softball into my late thirties, I never managed to hit a home run over a fence. I hit inside-the-park home runs, which are expressions of speed rather than power, but not once did I get to execute the home run trot that is the slugger's prerogative. No, I had to fly home. And I was an inconsistent defensive player, given to making errors on routine plays that undid the value of my occasional spectacular catch.

Still, I sustained the dream, tattered though it may have been by an occasional storm of self-knowledge, and avoided thinking about what I might actually want to do with my life. In my senior year of high school, when the time came for college applications, I understood that it was necessary to make some concessions to reality. Since I hadn't played for my high school baseball team as a junior or senior, because of lingering football injuries to my wrist and ribs, I realized that my plan to be discovered by a major league scout or a college coach was probably unrealistic. Unless the scouts or coaches came to watch me play recreation league softball and signed me up.

I made an appointment with the school's guidance counselor and asked her advice about college. She was, I can see now, remarkably kind. Questioned about my career plans, the only profession I could propose as an alternative to ballplayer came to me out of nowhere: I would be a physical therapist. I'd seen how much it had helped my father regain mobility after his accident, and remembered the therapist, Lee Turamo, coming to our house wearing a long white coat. Good, I'll be a physical therapist!

The counselor suggested I apply to Boston University, which had a strong program in physical therapy. But she pointed out that my college courses would include a lot of science, and my high school record in science wasn't particularly encouraging. Maybe I should also apply to a few small liberal arts colleges and take more time to make a career choice. What really sold me on the idea was her final point: I might be able to play baseball at one of these small colleges.

I was playing center field for the freshman team at Franklin and Marshall College, in Lancaster, Pennsylvania, when the fantasy finally ended. Neither the timing nor the place could have been better. A line drive was hit to the gap in right-center field; I dove and caught it, rolled over once, leaped to my feet to throw out the runner trying to return to first base, and the ball dribbled out of my hand as my shoulder seemed to lock in place.

Damaged ligaments and, eventually, a serious case of bursitis, had done what nothing else could. There would be no further need to dream of flying over the field of play wearing my pajamas. I could actually grow up, touch the ground, face reality's pitch.

The next semester, I took a creative writing class. For my first prose project, I returned to the material abandoned in 1957, when Mr. Lee punished me by assigning a composition on baseball. I wrote about the Brooklyn Dodgers moving to Los Angeles, discovering as I went along that I was writing about the beginning of the end of my baseball dream.

2

The Wink of the Zenith

I t was the fall of 1956, I was nine years old, and I was underfoot. My parents' bedroom floor, as they prepared to leave for a costume party, had become a football field over which I had complete dominion.

The Philadelphia Eagles were spread in a T-formation across the doorway, players' bodies frozen in postures captured by the Topps Company's photographers. Since I didn't have enough trading cards for a full Eagles lineup, the team had been bolstered by a few pickups from around the league. Similarly, the New York Giants, lined up on defense, included players not owned by the Giants but looking, in my opinion, sufficiently Giant-like. Lou Creekmur, a tackle for the Detroit Lions, was playing for both teams simultaneously, blocking against his own onrushing self. But this didn't bother me. I was owner, coach, referee, play-by-play announcer and color commentator, and, when the moment came, each player as well.

My parents, of course, were the fans, and they were not paying proper attention. They walked across the field, stood in the end zone, yammered about the length of the game. Dressed as a King and his Queen, the Royal Family, they freely and regally interrupted my game, trailing scents of Old Spice and April in Paris, behaving as though they owned the place.

Their television flickered in the background. It was a round-screened Zenith, like a big eye in the corner of the room. Though it was older and smaller than our boxy Philco in the living room, it was my favorite. My mother thought we ought to replace it, my father didn't like the shape of its image, my brother never watched it. But when light from the Zenith's eye started dancing, I believed that something inside was blinking at me. A presence from within the mysterious distances of Television was, I sometimes imagined, trying to send me a message, trying to reach me, share a vital truth. I welcomed the wink of the Zenith.

Now something strange was going on. As my father adjusted his cardboard crown and my mother drew thick black triangles around her eyes, I heard the announcer's voice from the television calling the action of my football game. I'd picked up the card of Adrian Burk, quarterback for the Eagles, and as I moved him backward for a pass, the announcer was saying, "Adrian Burk drops back to pass."

I didn't think I'd spoken out loud. But then the announcer said, "He's looking for Pete Retzlaff downfield," which was exactly what I'd planned for Burk to do, and I turned toward the Zenith.

A football game was being broadcast. From their distinctive helmet design, I could tell instantly that the Eagles were playing. Adrian Burk was throwing a pass on television, and Adrian Burk was also in my hand, and in my mind, throwing a pass. I repeated what the announcer said, "Oh, it's incomplete," then looked back and forth between the television and my hand.

A moment of utter clarity arrived: I could imagine something in the world of my head, and it could be entirely true! It could be what was broadcast on television, which was what happened somewhere else, real as the world. It was not that I made something happen on television simply by imagining it, but rather that my imagination could produce an alternate reality every bit as convincing as the one around me. And given what was around me, as the Royal Family showed off its broomstick scepters, I suppose that wasn't such a far-fetched conclusion. My powers were beyond make-believe: I could conjure a world and it would be real.

I looked over at the rest of my football cards, spread across the doorway on a field of carpet green as grass. My parents' beds rose above the playing field like bleachers. Then, moving in and out of the frame of my vision, my father the king looked like a team mascot. On screen, Ken Keller picked up three yards on a run up the middle. I crawled back to my game, but I didn't have a Ken Keller card, so I improved the scene: flush with my own capacities, I had Tank Younger, borrowed from the Los Angeles Rams, rumble for a touchdown as the stadium erupted in cheers.

When the Zenith was switched on, light exploded from a bright dot at the center of the screen. It filled the dark circle, crackling with static, then glimmered into vague shapes, black and white and gray, that took a moment to resolve. I loved to see the way this television woke up muzzy-headed and discombobulated, out of focus, not-quite-itself. It seemed to be letting go of its dreams, and if I were quicker I might have been able to see what they were.

I believed the dot was always there, though sometimes hidden by the closed eyelid of whatever mysterious presence was trying to communicate with me from inside the television. That was why I liked to invade my parents' room when they were elsewhere, and turn the set on. Liberate the eye.

Saturday was their usual night to go out. My brother was also out. As in an elegant dance, my costumed parents left just as the sitter, Mrs. Perler, arrived, and their hands touched briefly as they passed. Mrs. Perler settled in the living room with her knitting. Her cloud of hair was the same color as the smoke from her endless Lucky Strikes, which must have dyed it a matching gray over the years. I heard her needles clack as I moved toward the rear of the apartment, where the two bedrooms were. I waited in my room, reading the backs of my baseball or football cards, or leafing through a Classics Illustrated comic book. Within ten minutes, I knew Mrs. Perler was asleep in mid-stitch, and I was free to tiptoe across the hall and turn on the Zenith.

At nine years old, I no longer believed for certain that my parents had left our apartment and rushed to the television studio so they could appear on screen, at 8:00, disguised as Jackie Gleason and Audrey Meadows, then as Sid Caesar and Nanette Fabray at 9:00. For one thing, the timing would be difficult, unless the CBS and NBC studios were secretly located near each other in Flatbush, instead of somewhere in Manhattan as advertised. But the shows were on back-to-back, and my parents would get home an hour or two after *Caesar's Hour* ended, and I knew they liked to wear costumes, and they behaved so much like the Kramdens and the Hickenloopers, that I couldn't completely discredit the idea.

On *The Jackie Gleason Show*, when Ralph Kramden yelled at Alice in their Brooklyn apartment, threatening to send her to the moon with one punch, the voice was my father's. When Alice turned on Ralph, menace in her voice and body, she was my mother, balled fists and all. My mother's best friend, who lived right above us in the apartment building, looked exactly like Alice Kramden's upstairs neighbor and best friend, Trixie Norton. And I couldn't swear that my father's pal from the chicken market, Lefty, wasn't actually Ed Norton without the funny hat. Next, on *Caesar's Hour*, Charlie Hickenlooper stuttering in rage and frustration over Doris's schemes could have been my father standing in our living room any night of the week. There was something in Mr. Hickenlooper's raised voice, a growl that often turned into a cough, which was so characteristic of my father that I cringed when I heard it.

But I knew it couldn't be true. My parents were attending a costume party at the home of my mother's cousin, as they did every year near Halloween. They were wearing flowing robes and funny headgear, and talking in strange accents. So my parents weren't the people I saw on the Zenith behaving exactly like my parents.

However, the family had already been on television once. At least I thought we had. On a Saturday evening, a year or two ago, my parents took me to the CBS studio in Manhattan, where we were in the audience for the weekly game show *Beat the Clock*. Contestants were selected from the studio audience, and I remember my father's hand going up when blonde Beverly Bentley walked by. She knelt before him and they whispered together. She nodded, shook his hand. Then, once the show began, my father and I were up there as contestants on stage with Bud Collyer. I remembered my father setting off small mousetraps with a hot dog tied to a fishing pole while I crawled around the stage, undoing the traps after him. We completed six and earned the right to move to the next round. That's where I got to throw cream pies at my father, trying to hit the cigar stuck in his mouth. I hit his shoulder, grazed his cheek, then got the cigar and his whole face on the third try. So we went to the Bonus Round, where my father had to blow up and tie off balloons, which I stuffed inside his baggy coat. It was all unforgettable, down to the smallest details of how those balloons sounded and smelled when I handled them. But my parents have told me over and over that we never were on the show. That I made the whole thing up. Yes, we went to the studio to watch, but my father didn't volunteer. We stayed in our seats, though I wanted to get up and pee in the middle of the show.

My father wasn't on *To Tell the Truth*, either. That entire segment where he was all three contestants, each claiming to be Harry Skloot and testifying to various aspects of my father's life, each answering questions from Kitty Carlisle and Polly Bergen and Hy Gardner, each looking at each other before pretending to stand up at the end and identify himself as the real Harry Skloot: never happened. I made it up, too. A dream. But that was much later, thirty years after my father died in 1961, when I was trying to remember what he was like, and turned back to glimpse him on the winking Zenith once again.

When I switched the Zenith off, the picture seemed to fold in on itself. Then a star formed in the screen's center, thin legs reaching toward the darkening far corners, and suddenly vanished, leaving an afterimage I could see even with my eyes shut. Sound lingered too, a faint hiss. Pretending to be blind, I moved across the hall to my bedroom, arms extended, but secretly holding on to the vision of that vanished star.

There was one program my family watched together: *The Ed Sullivan Show*, on Sunday nights at 8:00. We gathered in front of the Philco in the living room, despite my requests that we watch in their bedroom. But the mood was always edgy, and inevitably one or the other of us split off from the group in front of the television. When circus acts came on, my brother got up, shook his head, and walked into the kitchen for a snack. If an animal act appeared, my mother stormed away, muttering "Filthy animals, who cleans up after them?" as she went into the kitchen to clean up any crumbs my brother had left behind from his snack. Novelty acts, especially the sight of the Italian mouse puppet, Topo Gigio, drove my father nuts, and he erupted from his easy chair to find a fresh cigar in the bedroom before he had to hear the toy's squeaky voice say, "Kees-a me, Eddie!"

I seldom left my place. The strangest moments, for me, were when Jackie Gleason or Sid Caesar appeared, especially if they appeared with Audrey Meadows or Nanette Fabray and performed skits as the Kramdens or Hickenloopers. This was really too much. My eyes shifted from the screen to my parents and back, and I didn't dare leave the room though I wondered whether they'd be on the Zenith too, if I turned it on in their bedroom. And if my parents sitting in the living room weren't actually on the screen before my eyes, reprising their domestic roles before a live audience, maybe they'd written in to Gleason and Caesar with suggestions on how to make their arguments more authentic.

I remember once I was terrified enough to run from the room when Jackie Gleason appeared on *The Ed Sullivan Show* in his role as The Poor Soul. Timidly, he tried to gather a meal for himself at the Automat, selecting a piece of pie from behind one of the glass compartments. He inserted his nickel in its slot, opened the small window, reached inside, and some unseen force behind the wall grabbed The Poor Soul's hand and tried to yank him through the window. Oh, how Gleason screamed! Eyes opened wide, mouth agape, hand trapped, his legs flailing as he dangled from the wall, he was more than I could bear to see. I'd eaten at Horn & Hardart's Automats many times. What happened to The Poor Soul was what I feared happening to me, had dreamt about, worried about. Now I saw, as in a nightmare brought to life, that I was right to worry. But how did Jackie Gleason know about my fears? This was, surely, further evidence of my parents' connection with him. They were so annoyed when I told them I didn't want to go to Horn & Hardart's that they'd called Gleason and added it to his act. It must have been that, because I was too mature to believe the substance of my fears had been glimpsed by the watchful eye of the Zenith.

In the fall of 1957, when we moved from Brooklyn, the Zenith was relinquished. But in the new, larger room my brother and I shared, we had a television of our own: a small, 1956 black-and-white Zenith portable that could fit on a tray. Its screen was rectangular instead of round, but almost the same size, and if we had to abandon the old one, I don't believe my parents could have purchased anything else more suited to easing my transition to a new home.

I still maintained the fantastical reciprocity between my imagination and television. Especially a small black-and-white Zenith television with lousy reception. It was as though these machines were a visible manifestation of my internal creative apparatus, a means of affirming that what I fabricated in my head could have a life of its own, and I still needed that outward assurance.

But once we moved, the connections became complicated. For instance, both *The Jackie Gleason Show* and *Caesar's Hour* were gone from television in the fall of 1957. It was as though I'd abandoned them with the old Zenith, left them trapped behind its blinking eye. Gleason's show would return to prime time in October 1958 and endure for more than a decade; Caesar would briefly return for five months in 1958, too, but was essentially finished as a television regular. I didn't believe that what happened to Gleason and Caesar in 1957 was truly my fault, but when we moved from Brooklyn that year, my television allegiances shifted. So did my imaginative connection. Instead of seeing my family's secrets given form on screen, I saw my own secrets blossom there. Not only that, but I began to understand that operating solo, relying only on my own imagination, might someday be sufficient.

It began with Will Paladin. Paladin was the cultured gunslinger from San Francisco, the lone crusader dressed in black, the moody mercenary whose card said "Have Gun, Will Travel." He had a mysterious past as a Civil War cavalry officer who graduated from West Point, a life back East from which he'd exiled himself. Home base was a hotel, and the only person in his life was a hotel messenger named Hey Boy, who brought Paladin correspondence from new clients. Grimly, willing to do what needed to be done in the interests of justice or mercy, an ethical Aristotle-quoting righter-of-wrongs, Paladin gave up his good wine and fancy food, growled some passage from Shakespeare or Keats, and rode off on his own.

Now here was the stuff of dreams! I was drawn to the Paladin Way as to no other cowboy hero of the time, Bret Maverick, or Jim Hardie on *The Tales of Wells Fargo*, Wyatt Earp, Matt Dillon on *Gunsmoke*, Sheriff Clay Hollister on *Tombstone Territory*, Flint McCullough on *Wagon Train*, Don Diego de la Vega on *Zorro*. Fine fellows, all. But none had the peculiar mixture of gravity, sensibility, elegance, alienation, and depressiveness that marked Paladin for me. He had no home, just a hotel room, which he didn't share with his brother, and he had no friends or kin to reckon with. The world as Paladin imagined it contained all sorts of sensual and intellectual possibilities, food and brandy and women and literature and gambling, but it was tainted by betrayal, violence, corruption. He read the papers, found stories of these evils, sent off his card. And when summoned, Paladin had no choice but to act, setting aside the higher pleasures for the higher calling.

What was there not to like? Except for the killing, of course, even if the victims deserved their fate. But by then I was sophisticated enough to know the killing on *Have Gun, Will Travel* wasn't real. Why, I'd seen actors die at Paladin's hands and appear a month later on some other show.

Have Gun, Will Travel debuted in the fall of 1957, on Saturday nights at 9:30, just when I would have been watching the last half of *Caesar's Hour* in my old Brooklyn days. Television had taken care of me after all, offering me something new, guidance or confirmation as I left our forsaken home—the small apartment in Brooklyn— and gone rambling on the sands of Long Island, singing Johnny Western's song, "Ballad of Paladin," as the waves broke. Followed my own calling. Depended on no one. Imagined the world a better place and then gone to make it so. Paladin was someone whose spirit I'd conjured up for myself, though it took television to give him substance. And to cast Richard Boone, which encouraged me to believe that a man didn't have to be handsome to be the hero of his own imaginings.

It wasn't far from Paladin's solitary adventures of the 1870s to the modern-day escapades of suave Peter Gunn, private detective. Dark suits, dark eyes, dark nights. I knew that Gunn's time and Gunn's mode were my time and mode. He knew the truth behind secrets. He imagined motives, and saw what was before his eyes. He had style. Peter Gunn was a more plausible projection for me: more flawed than Paladin, needing occasional help from Lieutenant Jacoby in eluding danger; less isolated, because he had a jazz-singing girl-friend, Edie Hart. I didn't want to be a private detective, but I knew that Gunn's work was really about being an observer. About impro-visation and the offbeat. For the ironically named Gunn, wit rather than weaponry was what worked, flair rather than fists. Violence wasn't the way to reach the heart of the matter.

As the 1950s ended, and I entered my teens, imagination got a jolt of hormonal distortion. The vertical hold went wild. I couldn't steady the picture. In flashes, I saw myself as a football player, de-spite being only five four and weighing 140 pounds, then as a singer, a heartthrob, a writer, an acrobat, a comic, a ventriloquist. I surely had the derring-do to walk a high wire or tame big cats. I was back to *The Ed Sullivan Show*, since the variety program was the best fo-rum for my multifarious self-inventions. I watched Perry Como's hour, Dinah Shore's, Garry Moore's. The Zenith was unreliable. I learned to adjust it from moment to moment, move it from place to place, talk to it, never give in to the urge to slap its sides when the picture wouldn't come clear.

Then, after my father's death and my brother's marriage, I moved with my mother to a beachfront apartment located on the flight path to Idlewild Airport. Soon she began going away on cruises, trying to find herself a husband. I was left alone, often for a month at a time, and at seventeen became transfixed by a character named Napoleon Solo on a new show called *The Man From U.N.C.L.E.* Everything about this show lacked credibility except the debonair American superagent, whose moves and attitude seemed to be copied from my own imagined moves and attitude. I considered changing my name from Skloot to Solo, which, I felt, would make matters more consistent. Floyd Solo. I spent Tuesday nights watching *The Man From U.N.C.L.E.* As planes passed overhead, reception on the Zenith became fuzzy and distorted, and it was impossible to hear anything except engine.

Halfway through my sophomore year of college, I came home from Lancaster because I had a ticket to see *The Ed Sullivan Show* at the CBS Studios in Manhattan. It was a lark and it was a farewell, because I no longer needed the Zenith as moderator. Discarded, the old set sat in the bedroom closet of the apartment where my mother lived with her new husband.

Going away to school had provided a series of clarifications and the right conditions for a fertile imagination to flourish. Okay, I was not going to be a professional ballplayer. But I discovered a passion for reading and began acting, then writing poetry. My classes gave me all sorts of useful structures for doing what I'd never been able to avoid doing: trying to make sense of my memories and dreams, my real experience and imagined concoctions. In English class, for instance, I learned about "objective correlatives," those objects or situations that T. S. Eliot viewed as the only viable way of expressing emotion. So I saw that bursitis in my right shoulder could correlate to the stiffened joints that held my athletic fantasies together, and by focusing on the localized pain I could accept the generalized pain of lost sports hopes. I was beginning to organize the internal clamor.

As I waited for *The Ed Sullivan Show* to begin, I felt a real sense of distance from its production. As a child at home watching it, I'd felt so connected, so alert because of the reciprocity I felt between my subjective life and the show's objective razzmatazz. Now, it was just performance. Performance sans illusion, too, as I watched a group of acrobats, The Seven Staneks, work hard to balance one another. I could hear their grunts. The banjo-playing band, Your Father's Mustache, seemed as far from my life as that Brooklyn apartment where my first ten years cascaded shapelessly forward. The Woody Herman Orchestra, however, sounded like the soundtrack to those Brooklyn years. Enzo Stuarti singing an aria from *I Pagliacci* was, maybe, part of a life I was moving toward, but it just made me feel embarrassed at all I didn't understand. I'd paid a lot of money for this fiasco!

But then came the comedians. Suddenly, the barriers came down and I was once again part of an exchange, living within the artistic experience. I was being shaped as I saw raw life given shape before my eyes. The Smothers Brothers sang "John Henry" and snapped at each other. Their contentiousness was milder than my brother's and mine at our best, but of course this was a public appearance, so they had to tone things down. I recognized something so personal in their act that at first I didn't even laugh. When George Carlin came on, I laughed though I recognized nothing personal at all. He was Al Sleet, the Hippy Dippy Weatherman, who gave the forecast for overnight: "Dark." He offered comment, attended closely to language and its potential to explode with hidden meanings, seemed both lost and in control, present and utterly absent.

Leaving the theater, I too was present and absent, here and elsewhere. It was a cold evening in late January, and I had to get down to Penn Station in time for a train to Lancaster. I could see my breath whisked back over my face as I walked fast into the wind. The light was that wintry black and white and gray, cornered among all the buildings, and I sensed myself adrift over the waters of the Upper Bay between Manhattan and Brooklyn, caught between the boy I was in his parents' bedroom, before his winking Zenith, and the young man here where the broadcasts originated. Like Carlin, I was both befuddled and clear, lost in the world but finding myself, a cynic and naif, entranced by what language was beginning to unveil for me. I was coming together, and finding my place, too. The place I believed I was finding was, as for all my great childhood heroes, an outsider's place. But not too far outside because I needed reception. I needed a clear enough picture.

3

The Summer of the Vampire

I n mid-July 1958, when I was eleven and attending Camp Rosemont in the Pocono Mountains, I was diagnosed with leukemia. The camp director phoned my parents in New York. It seemed as though they arrived in upstate Pennsylvania immediately after hanging up.

I'd spent the previous five days in the infirmary, kneeling on the bed and watching through a screened window as my friends crisscrossed campus on their way to meals or the lake or the recreation hall or the ballfields. Cabins where everyone else lived were arrayed in a loose circle, with the infirmary building outside like a moon in its orbit. I seemed to be a million miles away from normal life already, expelled from its gravitational force by whatever was wrong with me. I kept a small transistor radio perched on the sill. Over and over, I heard "All I Have to Do Is Dream," "Tears on My Pillow," "Summertime Blues," "Poor Little Fool," like the soundtrack to a movie called *Woe Is Me*. It was easy to feel sorry for myself.

My brother, almost nineteen, was a camp counselor that summer, and visited me every evening after dinner. Philip smuggled in extra desserts, then sat on the edge of my bed eating them since my appetite had dwindled. He tried to cheer me up by reporting about all the activities I was missing. Scattered throughout various bunks, some of the nine Skloot cousins would also find their way to the infirmary, spending a few minutes with me, smelling of energy and the woods.

But I was lonely and bored there, unable to focus on anything except the movement of healthy kids outside, the flow of play. *Go, go, go Johnny go!* Time had stopped dead, my first lesson in the peculiar dynamics of long-term illness. When my health failed to improve, the camp director sent me to the Wayne County Hospital for blood tests, accompanied by Philip. After we returned, time suddenly came back to life, and before I realized what was happening, my parents were standing beside the head counselor's shack, my packed trunk was ready to be shipped home, and people were waving good-bye.

My mother cried when she saw me. My father put his arm on my shoulder and squeezed, looking away toward the woods. I didn't want to go home, since the summer was only a few weeks old and I was sure I'd get better soon, but I could tell from their expressions that there was no room for negotiation. *Yakkety-Yak, don't talk back.* On the long drive to New York, my father rambled on about the Dodgers and their first season out in Los Angeles. My mother didn't tell him to shut up. So I knew I must be seriously ill.

Actually, I already knew. There had been enough partially overheard, whispered conversations in the infirmary hallway, and that unprecedented visit to the hospital, and a look on my brother's face that had alarmed me. But I never dwelt on those intimations, or on my growing sense of feeling sicker rather than better as time went on. And I didn't get truly frightened until my father got to talk about ol' Gil Hodges and Duke Snider without my mother calling him a Stupid Idiot!

As we approached the ocean, I calmed myself by counting bridges we crossed. The closer we got to Long Beach, the more exhausted I became. But by the time we were over the Atlantic Beach Bridge,

I knew I was going to die, despite my efforts at denial, and that I had been taken over by a *one-eyed, one-horned, flying purple people eater.*

We'd moved from Brooklyn to Long Beach about nine months earlier, and we had a new family doctor. He was the son-in-law of my parents' friends, the Kronenbergs, had gone to Harvard Medical School, interned at Massachusetts General Hospital, was an expert on blood disorders, and had opened his practice earlier in the year, just a few blocks from our house. I was allowed to call him Matthew instead of Dr. Gelfand. In the car, my mother kept calling him a Dream Come True.

Matthew was waiting for us at his office, where we went even before going home to unpack. He was tall, handsome, charming, and I thought he looked like Nick Charles on *The Thin Man*, which I could watch even though it was on at 9:30 because there was no school the next day. Nick Charles had been a Detective before retiring to be a Socialite, so I decided that Matthew would certainly be able to figure out how to make me better, to track down the culprit-germ and take care of him.

My father handed Matthew a fat envelope that the camp director had provided, containing the medical report that included the blood tests from Wayne County Hospital. Matthew sat on a stool that was too small for him, leaned over a desk that was too small for the report, and began flipping over the pages. He snorted twice, and I wondered if he was sick too. He frowned and shook his head, which seemed like a bad sign.

Then he examined me. I had the sore throat marked by pus, the swollen lymph nodes and liver and spleen. I was pale and fatigued, bruised where my father had gently touched me. I was yellowish here and there, and swollen in places that I hadn't known could swell, like under my arms or around my groin and eyes. *You give me fever!*

According to the lab report, my white blood cells were abnormal, particularly the lymphocytes.

I had so many telltale symptoms. But I didn't have leukemia.

"Harry, Lil, listen to me," Matthew said, spelling it out. "Your son does not have L-E-U-K."

I was shocked to realize that I understood what he was trying to hide from me. The word I'd heard whispered for the last week but refused to acknowledge. Leukemia, I knew, was very bad. So I hadn't allowed it to enter my conscious mind, transformed it into *Luke Easter*, first baseman for the Cleveland Indians. I still owned his 1954 baseball card. Sure, a nurse and a doctor whispering that I had Luke Easter. "L-E-U-K" also became big Luke from *The Real McCoys*, who moved with his grandpa Amos from West Virginia to settle on a ranch in California. Became Robin Luke and his new hit, "Susie Darlin'." *I thought you knew-ooo-ooo.*

My father took off his glasses and rubbed his face. He sighed, a sound I'd never heard him make before. My mother got furious. She turned to glare at me, and said to Matthew, "Then what does he have, that they needed to send him home from camp?"

"I'll have to do another blood test. But I'm sure he's got infectious mononucleosis."

"Oh my God! That sounds worse than You Know What."

Matthew shook his head. "It's not." Then he touched my cheek, smiled, and said, "Who have you been kissing, young fella?"

I asked Matthew to write it down: MONONUCLEOSIS. On the ride home from his office, I tore the word apart and rearranged its pieces: ME, NO, MESS, MUSCLE, CLUES, ISLE. UNCLE! My parents were strangely quiet in the front seat. Cigar smoke mingled with cigarette smoke, swirled in the hot trapped air, and sank over me. OMEN, SOUL, SOON, LOON, COUSINS.

With my brother still away at camp, I had a room of my own for the first time in my life. And I had to stay in it, not get out of bed except to go to the bathroom, for at least the next two months. OMINOUS, SECLUSION, COOL.

My parents put the portable television on a small, wheeled cart and left it beside my bed. The transistor radio fit between my mattress and headboard. I had magazines, comics, a few books, a shoebox full of baseball cards strategically placed around the bed. The room's two small windows were on the walls opposite my bed, so I couldn't watch the outside world as I had from the infirmary at camp. But I could gaze down the long hallway to the living room, watch as my mother or father moved from room to room. For the first few days, though, all I wanted to do was sleep.

Sometimes I couldn't tell if I was dreaming or was really back at camp or was awake but lost in fantasy. I heard reveille. I saw the American flag being raised on its pole, all campers in a large circle with hands over their hearts, the flag flapping in morning wind. I smelled hot cereal and burnt toast from the mess hall. I hit a line drive to right-center field and stretched a double into a triple. Swam before lunch. I even wrote a letter home, during rest-hour after lunch, saying I felt fine. I played basketball, sang camp songs, took a nature walk, lay on the grass in front of my bunk as darkness fell. *Where are you, little star?* And what I began to understand was that these mingled dreams and fantasies were making me sad. Though I couldn't find words to express what I felt, it was clear that thinking about what I'd lost was making me feel worse than the virus that had started all this. I had to let go of camp, find other things to occupy my imagination. I had to learn how to be this sick. SOLO, COSMOS, COINS. MUSIC. I continued to be obsessed with the game of "Words In a Word," focusing only on the long, intimidating name of my illness, finding within MONONUCLEOSIS such things as ONIONS, LEMONS, LIMES, MELONS, LION, COON, MOUSE, MULE.

Every Monday, a man came from the laboratory to draw blood.

His name was Mr. Pryor, which I quickly converted to Mr. Vampire, then to The Vampire. He loomed in the long hallway, dressed always in a black suit, black tie, black socks and shoes, white shirt. No stripes on the tie, no white handkerchief in the breast pocket, no watch fob looped from the buttonhole. His black hair was slicked back and his collar was often up in back, as though he'd put the jacket on hastily after getting out of his car, and it gave him a hooded look. He swooped toward me, that white shirt the only source of perspective, and after the first visit, I had to work hard not to cry as he approached. *Soon he'll be there at your side.* UNCOILS, SMILES, NOOSE, CUSS. *Have gun, will travel, reads the card of a man.*

Moving my desk chair over to the bed, setting the television on the floor so he could use its cart as a tray, The Vampire sat close and tried to chat as he opened his black bag, spread a cloth, and laid out his instruments. He noticed my baseball cards and asked who I rooted for. He noticed my radio and asked if I liked Perry Como. He saw my Hardy Boys books and my comics, and asked if I'd ever read Mark Twain. I tried not to look at his needle and syringe lying there on the cart, gathering afternoon light. He would tie a rubber strap tight around my biceps, spray a freezing mist on the crook of my elbow that stung but then left me numb, and draw out the blood. Then he would snap loose the rubber strap, bend my elbow up over a cotton ball, slap on a Band-Aid, and sweep from the room. I could hear his wings flap.

Now and then, Matthew would stop by to feel my spleen and liver. It hurt when he pressed hard under my rib cage and asked me to breathe in deep. He snorted his snort and asked how I felt. SLIME, MINUS, MOONLESS. My mother, standing just behind his shoulder, informed Matthew that I became excited watching baseball games and cowboy shows, and wondered whether I'd get better faster if she took the television away. He winked at me and said he didn't think so.

It didn't take long before I wondered why no one told me how I was doing. What were the blood tests showing? Why did my fever spike every afternoon? Was my spleen going to explode? Was I going to turn chartreuse now that the yellow was fading? COLON UNCOILS! CONSUMES. August grew thick and slow, even with breeze from the nearby ocean, and stopped passing altogether.

As far back as I could remember, I'd been sent to sleep-away camps in the Poconos for eight weeks every summer. There's a photograph in my family album that shows ten young boys in white tee shirts and shorts, all seated on a long bench, hands folded in laps, socks sagging around dark leather shoes. I'm in the middle of the row, with my feet, like the feet of three others in the photograph, not quite touching the ground. I've written the word "Me" across my chest with a pencil. There are five counselors standing behind us; a sign on the ground says Camp Equinunk, 1952. That was the summer I turned five.

So I didn't recall ever being at home or with my parents during a summer. I'd never seen how they behaved together when the weather heated up and their home was their own. Did they get along more peacefully, as I imagined, when my brother and I weren't there to bother them? Did they take walks or play cards or watch television together?

I also didn't recall being at home all day, day after day, in the company of my mother. That hadn't happened for the last half dozen years, since I started kindergarten after coming home from that summer at Camp Equinunk. The prospect had worried me, since there would be so much more opportunity for her temper to flare, her rages to erupt in violence. Matthew had said that one reason I needed to stay in bed was the risk of a ruptured spleen if I played like a normal eleven-year-old boy. Once, at the end of my first week at home, my mother took my temperature, read the results, and slapped me across the face. What if she pushed me into the wall or punched me in the belly?

As the days went by, I found myself watching carefully everything that went on in the house. I felt like an invader, an outsider, someone dropped into the midst of these strange beings. And by almost-false pretenses, since I wasn't in fact fatally ill, just inconveniently ill. If I had to stay in bed for a month or two, then I had to be waited on, as my mother described it over and over during her many phone conversations, and that was not how she wished to spend her summer.

This wasn't how I wanted to spend the summer either. In the first week, I worked out a routine, studying my baseball cards and sports magazines first, then playing a dice baseball game I'd invented, then watching television. After lunch I read comics for a while, Hopalong Cassidy or my favorite, Aquaman, who could live underwater and call in the sea creatures when he needed help against his enemies, and who'd struggled so hard as a kid to master his great powers. I liked some of the Classics Illustrated comics, too, especially *Dr. Jekyll and Mr. Hyde*, with the cover image of a ghostly, leering Hyde rising from the vapors of a green drink to hover over the doctor's head, and *The Ox-Bow Incident* with its three cowboys seen through the frame of a thick noose. The late afternoons and evenings were given over to music and television, or a ball game on the radio. Dull, strange, sweltering, it was a time when the air seemed to weigh more than it should, when light hurt, sheets and blankets grew sharp, and the least sound scorched its way into my brain.

Soon I began to find unobtrusive ways to extend my time out of bed. Long soaks in the tub, for instance. *Splish splash, I was takin' a bath.* The bathroom had been specified as a place where I could be when not in bed, but my mother was vigilant, despite her complaints, and before long would knock on the door to demand what I was doing in there so long. *Rub dub, just relaxin' in the tub.* Sometimes I ate a meal in our kitchen rather than in bed, an exception I'd dreamed up by saying I might spill my soup if I ate it in bed. Soup in the summer? Well, it got me out of bed. Then there were times when my mother actually left the house to shop or visit with a friend, and I was on my own. I would drift from room to room, keeping my hands to myself to avoid leaving evidence, but loving the sense of movement. I risked standing on the front porch, conscious of the time so that my mother didn't return and catch me.

The thing that surprised and frightened me was that I didn't feel like running, didn't yearn to ride my bike or throw a ball against the garage door. I wondered how long this would last, whether I would ever feel up to the activities I'd lost, the freedom, the ease and vitality. Whether I'd been transformed. OILS into SOIL, LINENS into MUSLINS. My body seemed to know what it needed, but I wasn't sure I agreed.

As August neared its end, I'd seen enough to understand that my parents were, in fact, always hostile toward each other. It wasn't just when my brother and I were around and active. I was present, of course, but stuck in the back room, not my usually intrusive self, and I saw that their fights were really not about me, even if my name popped up in the middle of the action. They were not caused by anything I'd said or done during the day that bothered my mother and led her to erupt at my father. He would come home from work in New York City, enter the house, and the arguments would begin as though triggered by chemical reaction. They always fought, even when they didn't speak. They never touched. They seldom spent time together except at the dinner table. COLISEUM, UNISON, LESSON.

I began to read the afternoon newspaper and a few magazines that my mother's friends brought for me when they came to visit. In that way, I came to understand that 1958 was the year of the V. There was the Van Allen belt, a zone of radiation encircling Earth that was discovered by a satellite, and then there was a satellite named Vanguard. There was a pianist from Texas named Van Cliburn who'd won a big contest in Moscow, and Venezuela was a country where Vice

President Nixon got attacked in his car, and the Dodgers had an ancient pinch hitter named Elmer Valo. Over and over on the radio, I was hearing a song called "Volaré" by Domenico Modugno, and reading in the newspaper about an actress named Gwen Verdon in a movie about the Yankees.

And, of course, The Vampire. One Wednesday he swooped down the hall and alighted next to my bed with a book under his wing. He dropped it at my feet, said "Here, this is a book you'll like," then began his blood-drawing ritual. Unwilling to look at him or at his instruments, I stared at his gift, *A Connecticut Yankee in King Arthur's Court*. It was by Mark Twain. I'd read several of that author's Classics Illustrateds but hadn't realized he wrote regular books too.

By now, I was as afraid of the burning-freezing spray as I was of The Vampire's needle. I dealt with that by singing to myself one of the week's new hits. *Just a dream, just a dream.* I didn't want to be rude, but I couldn't listen or respond to The Vampire's questions till I heard the rubber strap snap loose and knew that the week's blood draw was over. *It's oh-only make believe!*

"He wakes up," The Vampire whispered, "and discovers that he'd somehow gone back thirteen hundred years, to England in the time of King Arthur and the Knights of the Round Table. Just like that, he's in a whole other life." After placing a Band-Aid over my elbow, The Vampire looked over at me and said, "What do you think about that?"

I shrugged. "Does he ever get back home?"

"Read the book and find out."

After I heard the front door close, and saw my mother drift into the kitchen, I picked up the book. It was long, but there were a lot of pictures, so it seemed like the next step up from a Classics Illustrated comic book. I was hooked right away. A guy gets whacked in the head, goes through a period where he doesn't feel or know anything, then finds himself totally removed from the world he recognized.

I might not have gotten whacked in the head, but everything else about this Hank Morgan's story seemed familiar to me. What would he do and how would he adjust?

Before dinner, I'd learned that Hank was already trying to take over the kingdom and shape it to his own interests. He became The Boss. Very clever. I didn't understand all the stuff about Knights Errant, or politics, or holy fountains, and some of the writing was baffling to me, but I knew Hank had the right idea.

I had to become The Boss of this place, this world of illness where I'd been stranded. My mother might be some combination of Morgan le Fay and Merlin, and my father might be the shadowy and subdued king, but that, I saw, left plenty of room for me to manage things for myself. Like Hank, what I needed to do first was figure out what I wanted. This, in itself, was a whole new way of seeing my situation. I was sick, and that limited my choices, but I did still have choices. I might even have choices beyond which program to watch or listen to, which thing to read or play with. "You can't depend on your eyes," Hank says, "when your imagination is out of focus."

Well, the main thing I wanted was to be healthy again. But Matthew said that would take time, and if I tried to rush my recovery I would only make myself sicker. I wanted friends to visit me, but my best friends were either still away at camps of their own, or on family trips, or staying with relatives. I wanted to spend more time out of bed! That was a good one. I realized that my mother was making me stay in bed all the time because I needed rest and had to avoid injuring my swollen innards. Suppose I told Matthew that I understood those things, and promised to rest wherever I was? In a chair on the porch or in the small backyard or in the living room where there was a larger television. Then he could tell my mother it was okay, and she would have to go along with his recommendation.

With Hank as my example, I started to make a list. Since I wasn't allowed to listen to my brother's record player, I wanted one of my own so I wouldn't have to listen only to the radio, and to songs that a disk jockey's selected. I wanted to have records of my own, too. *Rave On!* I wanted a new notebook so I could compile statistics from all the summer's dice baseball games I was playing. I wanted my mother to stop bringing her friends into my room so they could feel my swollen glands. It was as though reading about the displaced Connecticut Yankee had completed some kind of circuit in my brain, connecting my desires with my ability to speak about them, sparking the capacity to release my frustrations, to give them voice. I finished the book in a few days. Then I asked my mother to buy me a copy of another book, a real book and not a comic book, by Mr. Mark Twain.

The next time Matthew came to examine me, I asked him to show me, on the Visible Man Anatomy Model that I had in my closet, where my spleen and liver were. Together, we took the breastplate off the model, and I touched its organs, removed the spleen and liver, listened as Matthew explained their functions. I saw that snorting was a habit Matthew had when he spoke, not a sign of dismay. I asked him what was being found in the samples of blood The Vampire took, and how I'd caught my illness. Now, fifty years later, I can still remember the way he smiled at me then, ran his hand over my crew-cut head, and instead of teasing me about kissing, told me I'd probably eaten from a fork or spoon that hadn't been cleaned properly and had contracted the Epstein-Barr virus from it. I would, he thought, have to miss the first few weeks of school, but if I was careful, I could certainly go outside for a while every day.

The morning sun hit the porch where I sat in a plastic chaise longue the next day. I remember the sun, and the view of two lush trees across the street that I hadn't really noticed before. I remembered something that Hank Morgan said, and that had made me cry when I'd read it in my bed: "It was a soft, reposeful summer landscape, as lovely as a dream, and as lonesome as Sunday." But now, even though I was no less alone than before getting to sit on the porch, I didn't feel so lonesome, and wouldn't have cried over Hank's comment. About four weeks had passed since my parents arrived at camp to bring me home. The corner of my mind that had believed I was going to die now believed I was going to get well. But I didn't dwell on it, as I hadn't dwelt on dying. Soon, Philip would be home again, and would begin working for our mother's uncle in a Manhattan dress factory. Soon, I would be able to go to school, and it would be like Hank Morgan waking up again, returned to the America he'd left, changed for good by all he'd gone through.

The next Wednesday, I was ready for The Vampire. When I saw him at the far end of the hall, I realized that he didn't really swoop, but walked with his arm held out to one side under the weight of his black bag. I also saw that he nodded when he saw me, and wondered if he'd always done that. He pulled the desk chair over, began lifting instruments from the bag, and glanced as usual at my pile of things on the bed. Then he stopped. He reached over and lifted up *The Prince and the Pauper.*

"Ah," he said, "the boys who switch places with each other."

He hefted it once or twice, as though demonstrating the weight of a real book compared with a comic book, then put it down and went back to his work. When he reached for his numbing spray, I surprised myself by saying "I don't think I need that anymore."

4

Cover Stories

The sea's surface rippled in dawn light. A page of newspaper floated by me on the wind. Quiet except for the bugling of sea gulls, the small barrier island where I lived seemed so peaceful. But I knew it was an illusion. From my perch atop the beachfront lookout tower, I scanned east to west, land's end to land's end. Then I scanned from the horizon line to shore. There was no sign of Nazi U-boats.

This wasn't completely unexpected, since it was 1961 and World War II had been over for sixteen years. But that was no excuse for slacking off. Could we be sure Hitler was dead? And even if he was, were we really safe? Maybe the Russians would mount a sneak attack, storming the late autumn sands of Long Beach, New York, to get at the secret Nike missile base located near my high school. A dinghy full of spies would drift in with the tide, barely visible in the slate gray waves and peppery light. Here on the front lines, I was the only man who could thwart them.

I was fourteen and had just read Stephen W. Meader's novel, *The Sea Snake*, for the third time. It was the story of teenaged Barney Cannon and his hometown heroics during the war. Barney lived on a small barrier island five hundred miles due south of mine, where he watched the Carolina coastline for Nazis. His lookout post was a small shelter dug into the sand rather than a concrete column, and he had a radio to communicate with naval personnel while all I had was a wristwatch through which I pretended to transmit messages. But like me, Barney had no binoculars and had to rely on eyesight, vigilance, and tenacity in order to protect his community.

During the course of a few weeks, Barney participated in a deep sea rescue, helped blow up a U-boat, identified Nazi saboteurs living anonymously near the Carolina coast, got kidnapped and taken aboard a U-boat, traveled to a camouflaged German facility in the Bahamas, was forced to accompany the German crew on a mission from which he escaped just in time to thwart their plan to bomb Atlantic City, New Jersey, from offshore, and ended up meeting a grateful president at the nation's capital.

I could do that. All right, first I might need to hone my skills a bit. Barney was observant, resourceful, brave, and daring, capable of figuring out the mystery of a U-boat's oil-free engine or remembering the layout of a Nazi fortification in the Caribbean. He routinely saved people's lives, a true and modest aw-shucks hero. He could also, apparently, swim forever. Barney was unflappable. I knew I was easily flapped. I was impulsive, naive, foolhardy, and wild. As a defensive back on the high school freshman football team, I'd repeatedly flung my hundred-twenty-pound body at our opponent's hundred-eighty-pound fullback until he knocked me unconscious and into convulsions. Barney Cannon did not get creamed by the big guys and he did not have convulsions.

He knew things, was savvy. I was baffled by much of what I saw. Also obsessed by guilt over my father's death in a swimming pool accident a few weeks earlier. I could swim, maybe not as many miles as Barney with my clothes and shoes on, but I could swim and hadn't saved my father's life. The fact that I hadn't been within two hundred miles of where he died did not relieve my sense of responsibility. I believed that if I were competent in the way Barney

Cannon was, I might have found a way to be in that swimming pool at the moment my father needed me.

The important difference between us, the quality that made us virtual opposites, was that Barney paid full attention to the outside world and none, as far as I could tell, to his inner world. Paying attention, getting outside my own head, and gaining competence: that's what I thought I was spending my mid-November mornings working on, chilled to the core atop the lookout tower between Edwards and Riverside boulevards.

To enter the tower, I had to remove a decomposing rectangle of plywood meant to block the small doorway, then crawl inside and climb metal rungs lining the wall. It had taken me several mornings worth of false starts, of sticking my head through the opening and looking up at the faint square of sky visible through the top, just to muster the nerve to enter the tower. Dark and cold even in full daylight, it stank of organic rot, urine, and salt. The rusting rungs stained my hands.

There were a couple of landings on the way up, with gunnery slits through the concrete where I could peer at the ocean. Morning wind howled through those slits, ricocheting up and down the hollow interior. I knew it wasn't really the crying of ghosts, but it sure sounded like that. Used condoms littered the floor and massive graffiti genitals adorned the walls, documenting the tower's primary current function.

While I was up there, scanning for submarines and trying to pay attention to the outside world, I found myself remembering when I'd gone into this lookout tower for the first time. It was two years earlier, after reading *A Night to Remember*, Walter Lord's account of the sinking of the *Titanic*. The first character to appear in the book was a crewman named Frederick Fleet, a ship's lookout stationed high in the *Titanic*'s crow's nest. Having been warned to watch for icebergs, knowing himself to be "the eyes of the ship," Fleet saw before anyone else the oncoming iceberg that would tear into the starboard side. The iceberg was, in a phrase that chilled my twelve-year-old bones, "darker than the darkness." Lookout Fleet banged the warning bell three times, a sound that haunted me more than anything encountered in the stories of Edgar Allan Poe, even when issuing from the neighborhood ice cream truck. That morning two years earlier, my first time atop the tower, I heard three bells ring from somewhere on the dimly lit sea. It might have been a bell buoy bobbing out beyond the jetty, or the sound of a distant ship's loose chains clanging in the wind, or something I imagined. But I could have sworn that the tower where I stood was a crow's nest, the beach it rose from was the *Titanic*, and I was destined for a long cold night adrift in the frigid seas.

Reading, for me, involved a kind of contagion. If I were fully engaged by a book, there seemed to be no way I could protect myself from it. Rather than drag me inside its imagined world, a story would take up residence in mine, like a virus gaining access to my DNA. I read with flimsy boundaries, erratic immunity. It wasn't enough just to experience what a character experienced—Lookout Fleet's fear and his long night in a lifeboat, Barney Cannon's adventures at the beachfront—I was compelled to incorporate what I read into my daily life.

After a few weeks with no submarine sightings, I was too tired and cold in the mornings to keep up my watch. Also, my reading changed, causing me to wonder if I might be looking in the wrong place for a threat of danger. The Hardy Boys, Frank and Joe, made me realize that the three hundred–room, pink-colored Lido Hotel at the eastern edge of town was a hotbed of sinister shenanigans.

I wondered how I could have missed that. The Lido's looming hulk always seemed to blush guiltily toward rose in direct sunlight, as though caught hiding its secrets. Located on prime beachfront property about two miles east of the lookout tower, it wasn't far from my home, and I passed its street entrance when I walked back from school. Maybe this familiarity caused me to overlook the Lido's nefarious purposes. Smuggling! Drugs! Drug smuggling Nazis!

Passing itself off as a luxury resort, the Moorish-style structure with twin onion domes and widespread wings was built in 1929 by the mayor of Long Beach just after he lost a bid for re-election and just before the stock market crashed. Broken by its builder's run of bad luck, the Lido nowadays wore its gaudy paint and extravagant exterior like an aging actress. Well, I was not going to be fooled anymore.

I'd begun reading The Hardy Boys mystery stories, starting with volume one, *The Tower Treasure*. My father may not have been a successful former New York City detective, now in private practice, like the Hardy Boys' father. But like them I did, suddenly, want to be a detective, solve a mystery on my own, find clues. Rather than follow in my father's footsteps and learn to deftly slaughter chickens in the kosher manner.

Where better to encounter a proper mystery than in my town's own version of the Tower Mansion? In the Hardy Boys story, "Tower Mansion was one of the show places of Bayport. Few people in the city had ever been permitted to enter the place and the admiration which the palatial building excited was solely by reason of its exterior appearance." Why, the author could have been talking about the Lido Hotel in Long Beach. And then he was, and I was on the case.

All I had to do was find out what bad thing had happened inside the Lido's walls, so there would be a case to be on. My first clue was that the local newspaper was evidently part of the hush-up. So was my English teacher, who became a suspect when I cleverly suggested doing a research paper on the Lido Hotel and she denied knowing what went on there now.

There was, I'd heard, a retractable domed roof above the restaurant, allegedly to permit dining under summer stars. But I deduced the truth: it was there to permit an easy way in and out for spies dangling from helicopters. Without access to a helicopter myself, I would have to use a different method to get inside the Lido, which was protected from street entry by gates and a ten-foot-high pink wall. The Hardy boys' method for gathering clues wasn't specific enough for my purposes ("do a little spying about this place"). The best I could do was walk the street in front of the hotel, or the beach behind it, and study the barriers that kept me away. More practice in observation. Also, piece by piece over the winter, as the springtime detective season approached, I assembled my wardrobe: black slacks, socks, sneakers, shirts, gloves, cap. I also recruited a partner, my neighbor Jay, who was tall enough to boost me to the top of the wall and who was reading the Hardy Boys books to prepare himself.

I staged my raid just after nightfall on a Friday evening in April 1962. By then I'd seen *The Guns of Navarone* and read the novel, which enabled me to realize that the Lido Hotel was actually a Nazi intelligence stronghold with two massive guns hidden in the floor of the rooftop restaurant. That was yet another explanation for the retractable dome. It also explained the presence of a possibly German-accented security guard, whom I'd slyly asked for the time during one of my winter reconnaissance walks.

Jay, eschewing the black outfit and accompanying me, I think, to witness my behavior rather than to protect all of New York from invasion, kept whispering warnings. *Look out for that shrub! Why's that light blinking on the top floor?* He squatted at the wall. I climbed on his shoulders, and he stood, enabling me to grab the top and scurry over. I jumped down, landing as planned within a small cluster of trees. Jay remained outside the wall, but positioned close to the gate in case he needed to take out the guard. I moved slowly toward a service door that was often open to admit the evening air, a door I believed would lead me to the kitchen area.

That's when a huge Rolls Royce pulled up through the gate. It looked like all Nazi staff cars in movies, and its headlights caught me. I dodged into the darkness. Glare from bright lights above the Lido's door flashed off the car's windshield, and I felt seen by the secret enemy inside. Then I dashed through the gate the car had just entered, and raced past Jay toward home. He laughed as he ran behind me, but I knew I'd gotten all the proof I needed.

Spies, sleuths, scouts, shamuses: as an adolescent my literary heroes, like my television heroes, were the quiet watchers populating novels of adventure and intrigue. Like them, I practiced observation, taking in the world around me for the clues it offered about ominous signs, hidden threats, unexpected turns, intimate betrayals. The randomness of events would form a pattern, a story, and begin to make sense. At the time, I never wondered what drew me to such figures or made me identify with such deep vigilance. I just knew that reading about them was like seeing my way through the dark.

It was the Cold War era, of course, and popular culture was full of spies, full of secret agents and investigators and operatives. I saw the first James Bond movie, *Dr. No*, when it appeared in 1962, and read a few of the Ian Fleming novels in which Bond had regularly been featured since 1953. For years, I remained intrigued by my favorite detectives probing the abundant mysteries around them. I remember being transfixed at the age of seven by the opening announcement to a show called *I Led Three Lives*, as a man spoke of someone named Herbert A. Philbrick, who was simultaneously an "average citizen, member of the Communist Party, and counterspy for the FBI." Danger compounding danger, requiring layers upon layers of selves behind which to hide. False names, cover stories, safe houses. This stuff compelled my attention far more fully than stories of cowboys or soldiers or explorers or boys with their animal pals. Dapper or plain, fat or thin, brilliant or plodding, these men with their deep souls and clear purposes peopled my dreams, shaped my intentions, helped me define how I wanted to be in the world, though I had absolutely no aptitude for their way of life.

I knew at the time that I never felt safe in my house, but didn't connect that feeling with my passion for stories about ultra-competent observers, experts at concealment and control of their emotions, men who survived by stealth and vigilance and grim moxie. Those first years with my newly widowed mother were wild and explosive. So volatile and violent by nature, she now seemed transported beyond all restraint by the shock of my father's death and fear of the future. Her explosive rage, erratic and ferocious, could turn on me in a flash. With nothing and no one to constrain her, she would hit, kick, bite, all accompanied by growls and shrieks that sounded prehistoric. There was a madness to her behavior, I see now, but then it struck me as simply the logical next step up from her normal conduct. Sometimes as she perched on her dining chair in the kitchen, I thought of her as an armed missile, like the Ajax I saw at the Nike base not far from my school, poised and quiet for the moment but dangerous to be anywhere near. With her fabricated and vaguely European accent, sometimes I thought of her as The Mastermind of Chaos, a figure concocted from my readings in spy fiction and viewings of television and movies, not unlike Rosa Klebb, the Spectre agent played by Lotte Lenya in *From Russia with Love*. And though she never blamed me for failing to save my father, her behavior reinforced my sense of responsibility. The situation was my fault, and mine to handle. I spent as much time as I could away from home and her wanton wrath, or at home but invisible, in a kind of alternative life where there were no surprises and I was vastly skilled.

At seventeen, thanks to a birthday gift from my aunt Evelyn, I found someone who struck me as the perfect incarnation of the sort of character I most admired and wanted to be: Alec Leamas, from John

Le Carré's new novel, *The Spy Who Came in from the Cold*. Leamas knew what to do in a world gone mad. You faced things calmly. You dealt with The Circus, dealt with Control. You knew that what mattered was "the caring about little things—the faith in ordinary life." You longed for warmth and wanted to come in out of the cold.

I admired Leamas's bitter composure and his certainty in the face of the powerful, deceptive forces arrayed against him, forces that didn't care about him or about what they might have to do to him. Leamas wouldn't have bolted when faced with the Nazi car and the glaring light at the Lido Hotel, as he hadn't bolted from the East German arclight that found him at the end of *The Spy Who Came in from the Cold*. In fact, he'd have known such a car would materialize, and planned what to do when it glared at him. Moody, isolated, self-reliant, he knew what he knew, and he knew what he didn't, and he faced life accordingly. He was elusive, and Le Carrè wrote that "it was hard to place Leamas," but I thought I understood him. A short man with stubby hands and fingers, he looked like my father and like the man I was destined to be, but now I realized that his undistinguished looks were a help rather than a hindrance. His manner and appearance may have made him an anti–James Bond, but he was the more impressive and important to me.

In the summer of 1964, long finished with dawn trips to the lookout tower and reconnaissance raids on the Lido Hotel, I began running a few mornings a week along the beach instead. My high school football coach, Mr. Piazza, said it would be good for the legs and the wind, the best way to prepare for my senior season as a halfback. I ran west on the soft sand near the boardwalk, then turned around and ran east toward home on the hard sand near the tide line.

My job that summer was as a short-order cook at a beachfront refreshment stand operated by the Lido Hotel. Though it might have been the perfect setup, a real coup for the young spy, I wasn't there as an undercover operative. I had, in fact, discovered that it was possible to be like those heroes of mine without engaging in espionage or intrigue, without being a literal detective or spy. As decisions approached about where to attend college and what to study, this was an important discovery, freeing my ambitions from the grip of Barney Cannon, the Hardy Boys, and Alec Leamas. I wouldn't have to major in Spycraft and Counterintelligence, after all.

The book that revealed this to me was a baseball memoir, *The Long Season*, written by Jim Brosnan, a pitcher for the Cincinnati Reds. Throughout the 1959 baseball season, beginning before spring training, when he received his contract in the mail, and ending on the season's final day, when he left the clubhouse with a new contract in his hand, Brosnan watched his teammates, watched his opponents, watched the sportswriters who accompanied the team and the stewardesses on its flights and the fans at its games. He watched himself. He held himself apart while also taking notes in the bullpen, in the dugout or clubhouse, at night in his hotel room, anywhere.

The Long Season was the first book I'd ever read that was a true story told by the person in it, something I hadn't realized was possible. You could tell your own story! Traded to the Reds in midseason by the St. Louis Cardinals, Brosnan was treated by owners like an object, a piece of property, and when it came time to write his story, that's how he treated himself. With an intimate distancing, so that he could observe, report, assess, mock. I loved this book even before I reached Brosnan's entry for July 9, which seemed to see something essential about me as well as about himself: "When I get involved in a book my mind doesn't operate properly till I read my way back to reality."

I wanted to see myself and my life the way Brosnan did. Investigate myself, make sense of what was happening, find meaning in it. This could be done even while being a baseball player. Maybe, for me, it could be done better while being a baseball player, or whatever fit me best. And once I began to see myself clearly, maybe I should write about what I saw.

Brosnan was a good writer, I could see that right away, when he said in the book's early pages that fellow pitcher Sal Maglie "looks like an ad for the Mafia." I'd seen Maglie when he played for the Dodgers, and knew that Brosnan was not only right but funny as well. Probably even better as a writer than he was as a pitcher, though he was admirable at that too. And full of the kind of understanding that made it seem as though he were talking right to me: having struggled with the same issue on Saturday mornings when playing high school football, I understood what Brosnan meant when he said that "one of the first decisions a pitcher must make when he knows he's to pitch the second game of a Sunday double-header is what time to eat breakfast." This was much better than the stuff I was used to reading about sports, like this passage in John R. Tunis's *The Kid from Tompkinsville*: "He realized that more important than fielding or hitting, more important than anything, was that funny inner quality called courage."

I think that reading *The Long Season* made it possible for me to begin turning upon myself the skills I admired in the men I'd read about, the men I practiced being. Instead of yearning to look only outward, like Barney Cannon or the spies and detectives populating my imagination, I could begin to look inward with the skills of a cool, outward-looking intelligence operative. Observe myself and my life, as I would continue to observe the world, but with greater discipline and purpose. And live my life as well. That part was important. Be a player in the game I was writing about, like Jim Brosnan and baseball.

Then I discovered *The Loneliness of the Long-Distance Runner*. Alan Sillitoe's novella provided the first instance I can remember in which living a story and living my life came together. Like Colin, the seventeen-year-old thief who is forced to run and race while in a juvenile detention facility, "I knew what the loneliness of the long-distance runner felt like, realizing that as far as I was concerned this feeling was the only honesty and realness there was in the world and I knowing it would be no different ever, no matter what I felt at odd times, and no matter what anybody else tried to tell me." The pace of his thinking matched the pace of my running and thinking while I ran. He knew what I knew. I didn't have to read my way back to reality because what I read was simultaneously what I lived.

As I ran on the beach, I remembered Colin saying he'd never been as free or thought as clearly as when he was running. He was alone in himself and happy to be that way. He was also finding wisdom in himself, as I was.

Colin learned that "cunning is what counts in this life, and even that you've got to use in the slyest way you can." A few years earlier, I would have agreed with him. Now though, as I built my endurance and sharpened my vision, I was thinking that balance was what counted in this life, balance and the courage to find it.

I didn't have pressure to win a race, but I did have pressure from my mother to continuing living with her after graduation and attend nearby Hofstra College. In return, she'd promised me a new Ford Mustang. I knew I needed to get away, but my mother said that my getting away was actually an act of betrayal, of abandonment. She said I was free to go, but she also said that I shouldn't go, that I had responsibilities to her.

I can remember the moment when my decision got made. It was easy to remember because it happened just as I ran past the beach-front lookout tower on my way home. There was a voice in my ear, disguised as a seagull's bugle, and at first I thought it was my father. Then I realized it was Colin, or rather it was my own voice speaking Colin's thoughts when, just before choosing to lose his big race, he thinks, "Only if I take whatever comes like this in my runner's stride can I keep on keeping on like my old self and beat them back."

At summer's end I went away to college. My mother drove me to Pennsylvania, and saw me to my room in the dorm at Franklin and Marshall College. I waved as she drove away, and within six months was standing with her at her wedding to a man she met the night the new year began. I had not only declared my own freedom, and begun my own adult life, but by doing so had set her free as well.

5

Home Economics for Halfbacks

In the autumn of 1962, when my mother became a travel agent, she knew where Europe was relative to New York, and she could place the Caribbean. She might have been erratic when it came to American geography, to Minneapolis or Tucson or Nebraska, what was near what, but she believed these were areas where nobody traveled anyway, so why worry about them? As to Mexico or Peru or Turkey, she thought it was her business to convince people not to go to such dirty, dangerous locales, so there was no real need to situate them in her mind. And who would actually travel to Tahiti when they could buy a book of Gauguin's paintings instead? My mother figured she had the basic knowledge she'd need to get started in the travel business. The rest would follow if necessary.

She was fifty-two and had been a widow for one year when her old friend Sam Wolff called to suggest the job with the travel agency he owned. She'd never worked outside the home, had no training except for a few months of art school in 1925, and no income prospects other than the monthly checks her brother continued to send, a shadow of the salary my father had earned managing my uncle's dress factory. Sam Wolff, who still lived in the Brooklyn apartment building where I'd spent the first ten years of my life, had been shocked by my father's sudden death. He or his wife, Lola, would call my mother every few weeks to see how she was doing. They'd drive out to Long Beach to visit us some Sunday afternoons, worried about how my mother would fare on her own, saddled as she was now with a fatherless son of fifteen.

"As if being a widow wasn't enough!" she'd say, closing her eyes.

I remember Sam, perched beside Lola on our living room sofa, leaning forward to speak to my mother across the room. "Three days a week in the office," he said. "You can do the rest from home."

Then he'd lean back, and Lola would lean forward. "It's time you got back into the world, Lil. Life goes on."

Soon the dining room table was festooned with travel brochures, airline and cruise manuals, guidebooks. My mother brought a map of the world home from the office, unfurling it on the living room sofa when she needed to respond to a client's strange request. *I told her Brussels. But no, she insists on Luxor and Sharm el-Sheik. Can you imagine? Come help me find them on the map, make yourself useful.*

Brussels was her primary recommendation for anyone wanting to travel overseas. She had been there on her first trip outside New York, in 1928, to attend a cousin's wedding. Her only other travel was a honeymoon voyage to Cuba, and the less said about that the better.

Outgoing and flamboyant, my mother especially liked a travel agent's auxiliary functions. She would book clients on luxury liners to England, dress up in her most elaborate outfits, buy flowers, and rush to the pier to see them off. She loved the drama of departure, the whole World War II feeling of dockside farewells, champagne toasts, and moaning foghorns. It was making the actual arrangements that could be a bother, dealing with clerks and staff, functionaries. And there was always a flurry of last-minute details to check, worries about forgotten tickets and hotel accommodations, the freshness of a bon voyage cake, the contents of a complimentary travel bag from the agency, the adequacy of berths, the quality of food on board, the chef's training and experience, the aperitifs.

She began to spend long evenings on the phone, smoking

Chesterfields as she called relatives or talked to friends from Brooklyn, scouring her address book to re-establish contacts and suggest vacations. She said she was offering her services. *We call this marketing, young man. Listen to me and learn something.*

Her knowledge of tourism expanded. So did her finesse in covering up its gaps. *There's a marvelous beach on Carmina Burana.*

Her only real problem involved waking up at 7:30 three mornings a week. This was at least four hours too early for her, since my mother had always stayed up till 3:00 at night. She tried various stratagems: buying a second alarm clock and setting it for fifteen minutes after the first one; demanding that I wake her before leaving for school, then call home when I arrived at school, letting the phone ring until she answered it; asking a neighbor to knock on the door or the secretary from the travel agency to call from Brooklyn before leaving for the office. Nothing worked. She was routinely late, but Sam Wolff didn't care, and eventually my mother decided she didn't need to be at the office till afternoon anyway.

Soon she began taking advantage of the free or reduced price travel available to agents. She would go on cruises herself, debarking here and there, and bring me an odd assortment of swizzle sticks or coasters emblazoned with restaurant and hotel insignia. These were genuine business-related trips, but on the phone she would tell her confidantes that there was another purpose too. *It's time I met a fella.* She bought new clothes and packed away her *widow's weeds.* She lost weight. She worked on her piano playing and refurbished her fabricated British-Hungarian-Dutch-Russian accent.

Every few months, I would be left alone, usually for three or four weeks, with a cash allotment for groceries. *Behave yourself. Keep the apartment clean. No visitors.*

At fifteen, in early 1963, I was a high school sophomore who obeyed rules. I went to classes, did my homework and extra credit reports, sat in the same seat every day in the school cafeteria eating lunch with the quiet guys over by the far window. After the seasons ended, I turned in my football jersey or my baseball cap and didn't try to keep them as souvenirs. I didn't smoke, didn't drink, barely danced, and didn't have a steady girlfriend to dance with anyway. I even tried to adhere to my mother's sometimes cockamamie edicts, the trickiest being *Don't miss sundown services. And get home before dark!*

Just a few months earlier, in November 1962, I'd finally finished my routine of nightly bike rides to the synagogue, where I attended services in my father's memory. Every night for a full year after his death, I would show up at sundown and pray among the same ten or twelve old men, the regulars. Heads hidden beneath ragged prayer shawls, they mumbled through the Kaddish together as evening light set the stained-glass burning bush ablaze in the sanctuary wall. Most were mourning family members, friends, entire villages lost in the Holocaust. The first time I arrived alone at the synagogue, one week after my father was buried, they'd turned around to greet me with nods and blinks and murmured Yiddish phrases. They never spoke to me again, but always checked to be sure I was there before beginning to pray. I missed only two nights during the year of mourning: one when a blizzard prevented the other men from reaching the synagogue, though it hadn't prevented me, and the other when a freshman baseball game went into extra innings at a school across Long Island, and I couldn't get back in time. Coach Bloch had to sit with me on the bus, trying to get me to stop crying and convince me that my father's soul would still rest in peace. At first he thought I was crying because we lost the game.

It wasn't just the old men in the synagogue who didn't speak to me. Neither did the rabbi nor the cantor nor my father's two brothers, the ones who'd originally assigned me the task of those nightly prayers. I didn't understand why they were necessary, or what they would accomplish, but never imagined I could question my religious leaders, aged fellow mourners or bereft uncles. *Don't ask any questions. Just do what you're told.* But was my father's soul afloat in the afterlife, unable to rest unless I did my duty? Was his death some sort of punishment for which I was asked to atone? What would happen because I'd missed those nights? As the year passed, I found myself growing angry and resentful, and also increasingly sad, as though I were about to lose my father again, and for good, when the first anniversary arrived and my task ended.

I lived with my mother in a small apartment overlooking the beach, where we'd moved a few months after my father's death. I was no longer near my friends and didn't know anyone my age in our new building. Sometimes I liked to walk to my old neighborhood in the mornings, catching the school bus there instead of in front of my apartment. That, and the occasional walk on the beach, which my mother forbid because I might bring sand into the apartment on my shoes, were among my few rebellious acts. Before coming into the apartment, I would remove my shoes and socks in the building's basement, methodically de-sand them, and pick any leftover grains from between my toes.

Sports and rock 'n' roll were obsessions. I collected trading cards and forty-five-rpm records with equal fervor, and I used them, inventing games or scenes, losing myself in their worlds. When my mother was away, and the weather kept me indoors, I would cut the bottom out of a shoebox and tape the hollow rectangle above my bedroom door: a basketball hoop through which I'd shoot a pair of balled-up sweat socks. In the background, a stack of new hits. Or I sang along with the radio while pretending to strum my Stella guitar, which I'd kept behind my bed even after six months of lessons proved me useless as a musician. Occasionally, a song would come on and sabotage me: Shep and the Limelites singing "Daddy's Home" could reduce me to tears, even though I knew it was a silly love song and not about lost fathers at all.

I could do a wicked impression of Frankie Valli singing "Big Girls Don't Cry" in his crazed falsetto. My football teammates loved it, and I loved making them laugh. That winter, my left arm was in a hand-to-elbow cast because of a broken thumb sustained when I'd carried the football on an end-run and my free hand smashed into a tackler's helmet. I'd delayed revealing the extent of the injury, telling myself that Coach Piazza was right, it was just a bad bruise, playing two more games with it heavily and futilely taped. At the end of the second game, diving to catch a pass, I landed on my left hand and damaged it further. I'd finally gone to the doctor.

The break was slow to heal. My cast was soon dirty, covered in autographs and odd drawings, and the skin below itched all the time. I hated being unable to play, and had liked to hang around at prac-tice after school during the rest of the season, holding a ball in my right hand, cheering the guys on, talking for a moment or two with Coach Piazza as he walked around the field, trying to ensure that he wasn't angry with me for being hurt.

Before she left for her winter cruise, my mother shrouded the cast in Saran Wrap to keep it from shedding plaster. She told me to keep it covered till the doctor cut the cast off at the end of the month. One of the clearest indicators of my character as a fifteen year old is that I dutifully taped my cast in fresh plastic casing every morn-ing after I'd showered.

That winter of 1962–63 was the coldest in more than two hun-dred years. My mother complained because the frigid weather was ruining her European travel business, and no amount of Caribbean cruises could compensate for the losses. Christmas was lousy, New Year's was lousy, who knew when it would end? But she was glad to be heading south herself, on a cruise to the Bahamas. As always, she hoped to meet her fella, maybe a surgeon or film producer or an in-ternational banker fluent in four languages. Independently wealthy would be good. Descended from royalty would be better.

A cruise's destination didn't matter much to my mother, as long as the climate was warm. Cruise life reminded her of hotel life, which reminded her of the classic romantic films she loved, and the exclusive world of elegant rooms and fancy lobbies and chambermaids and quality service that had always been her model of the good life.

I remember that when she left in January, I turned on the radio in my room and, as though being reminded of my mother's warnings, heard Bobby Vee singing about the night having a thousand eyes. *Behave yourself. Keep the apartment clean. No visitors.* She'd know, believe me, she'd know.

But I didn't particularly want visitors. My home, my mother's domain, had never been a place I brought friends. Her demands for order and cleanliness, her surveillance techniques, the way she found evidence of damage when nothing more than breath had touched the furniture's surface, made the fallout from a guest's visit too stifling for me. I either played at a friend's house or in the street, or on a school team. My childhood friend, Johnny Frank, told me last year how strange it all seemed, saying "I had a fifteen-year-old friend who lived by himself! In a museum!"

That winter when I was fifteen, I found myself drawn to cooking. It was a risky attraction, like being drawn to surfing when you couldn't swim, but I was unable to help myself. I loved being in the kitchen, concocting, combining. During her travels, my mother wanted me to use the stove only to heat up frozen dinners, which held the least likelihood of leaving a mess inside the oven. No need to roast or bake while she was gone. She didn't want me to use the stove-top burners, either. No eggs, no bacon, no oatmeal. *Cold cereal is fine for breakfast every morning.* But since she didn't flat-out forbid cooking, and I was neat enough around the stove, and willing to clean up after myself, I began to experiment with simple and cheap dinner preparations as soon as I was on my own.

My main model was the finished dishes we'd get at my favorite

Italian restaurant, La Seranata. I knew how steak pizzaiola should end up looking and tasting, but not how it might get that way, and my first attempts relied on round steak drenched in a can of diced tomatoes and sprinkled with dried parsley flakes. I didn't think about garlic or basil or pepper. I didn't consider onions or oregano, didn't understand about using olive oil in a frying pan. So it was going to be easy for me to improve as the month went along.

At the end of January, I had an appointment with the orthopedist to remove my cast. I rode to his office by bike after school, carrying a paperback copy of Joseph Heller's *Catch-22* in my coat pocket. The novel had been on a list my English teacher handed out. Read the book, write a report, improve your grade ten percent. I hadn't expected to like it too.

I sat in the waiting room and read the chapter in which Lieutenant Scheisskopf is involved in the court-martial of Clevenger. The absurdity of those rules and catches ensnaring the characters, the impossibility of ever satisfying people in command, the way language ran amok, all made me laugh out loud as Clevenger was chastised for not saluting when not speaking to Scheisskopf. There were tears in my eyes when the nurse came out to escort me into the examination room.

"Don't cry, Floyd," the nurse said. "There's nothing to be afraid of."

"I'm not crying, I'm laughing."

She shook her head and suddenly it was as though I were living out a scene from the novel I'd been reading. Real life and fiction seemed to merge. Like my inventions in the kitchen or my fantasies involving music and sports, this too was the kind of concocting and combining that delighted me, so I laughed again. The nurse, unconvinced, patted me on the shoulder.

"It won't hurt," she said. "Trust me."

Coming home that evening, I stopped at Waldbaum's and bought myself a veal chop, a tomato, five mushrooms, and a small can of baby green peas. I remember standing in line among the grownups with their carts of groceries and thinking of myself as quite sophisticated. Pedaling the rest of the way home, I was shocked at how weak my left arm felt as I tried to hold the groceries and handlebars. But I was thrilled to have the arm liberated.

After a shower to remove caked-on dirt, I did my homework, then began to cook, throwing all the ingredients into a pan at the same time, waiting for the chop to stop being pink. I could barely grip the pan with my left hand as I stirred with my right.

My dinner tasted nothing like the veal served at La Seranata. Fortunately, the new school term was beginning, and I was enrolled in an elective Home Economics class: Chef's Course for Males, taught by Coach Piazza. Most of the starting football team was taking the class. We'd all said it would be good for team spirit and a way for us to improve our teamwork. We'd said it would truly be Learning, since none of us knew much about cooking, and wasn't that what school was for? We tried never to say it would be fun, or easy credit. So far, we'd met three times, and I loved it. We would begin actual cooking that week.

The classroom was set up like a science laboratory, but with large stoves instead of lab benches. During the first class, Coach asked us to work in groups of four at each stove. I joined with the other offensive and defensive halfbacks, and we went through the space to learn what everything in a kitchen was. We were warned about safety issues and emergencies. Our initial assignment was going to involve making a pizza from scratch.

I was the first to get to the classroom, claiming the central space in our little kitchen for myself. While we created and learned to knead dough, I thought about the mimeographed recipe we'd been given for tomato sauce, and was astonished. Carrot and celery in tomato sauce? And what exactly was nutmeg? Coach showed us how to peel a garlic clove, unwrap and dice an onion without crying, sauté. It was one revelation after another for four halfbacks in their aprons.

As the weeks progressed, we learned eggs and pancakes, ham steak, the difference between broiling and baking. We learned not to overcook vegetables or undercook sausage. Coach approached each dish the same way he'd approached each play during football practice: describe it out loud, walk through it slowly and deliberately with each person doing his assigned task, comment, then repeat at game-speed.

One night during the week, my cousin Emily called while I was cooking another piece of round steak. When I brought her up-to-date, she said she'd send me a cookbook, which made me laugh. I hadn't even thought about cookbooks, probably because my mother, if she'd had any, hid them as she hid her copy of *The Fifty-Minute Hour*, with its lascivious descriptions of sexual activity. Before the week was out, I owned a copy of *"The New York Times" Cookbook* and was trying to make a budget intended to cover a month's worth of frozen dinners stretch to cover my nightly culinary experiments.

Tomato sauce bubbles and splatters when simmering! So does olive oil! Eggs drip; pans get caked with scorched meat. My mother was right to worry about messes. I learned to cook with a wet dish towel draped over my forearm and a dry one over my shoulder, cleaning as I went along. The night before my mother returned from her cruise, I spent two hours scrubbing all the kitchen surfaces.

When I got home from school the next day, she was waiting for me. The oven door was open, the stove top grills were removed so that the naked and filthy burners were exposed, and all the cupboard doors were open. The room smelled of disinfectant and my mother's rage. She grabbed my left wrist and yanked me toward the stove. A sharp pain shot through the base of my thumb.

"How dare you?" she shrieked. "Because of you, I'll never meet a man!" Then she let go of my wrist and collapsed at the dining table. "You belong in an orphanage."

By early spring of 1963, I'd stopped taking the school bus home and would walk the two miles by myself. The route I had worked out allowed me to pass the house we'd lived in when my father was alive and the synagogue where I'd mourned for him. But I never tried to enter either building. I didn't know the new owners of our house, and felt sundered from the synagogue, repelled as though by a field of force. Most afternoons, I stopped across from the window with the stained-glass burning bush and looked at its dull exterior view, so unlike the flaming sunset seen from inside as the Kaddish began.

My mother's words stayed with me. *You belong in an orphanage.* So many clever retorts occurred to me in the weeks that followed: *I thought that's where I was!* Or *I'll give them a call!* Or, simplest of all, *Yes, mother.*

As I walked, I sang to myself, a mix of recent hits. Phrases from Skeeter Davis's song about the end of the world tangled with the Cascades's hymn to the rhythm of the rain and the Rooftop Singers inviting everyone to walk right in. There were snatches of Hebrew prayer, a riff from "Telstar" by the Tornados. All this musical cacophony was the score for thoughts about how to manage my life at home when my mother was between cruises. The more she was gone, and the more I grew accustomed to caring for myself, the harder it became to revert to being under her domination and moodiness. I developed plans intended to accommodate her terror of dirt or fire or disorder, whatever caused her list of unmanageable rules for our apartment, so her returns home might be easier to endure. I thought about how to handle the tricky economics of my food budget.

I was, I see now, one very strange fifteen-year-old boy. More and more, my fantasies abandoned sports or music, turning instead to home economics, home management. All my old supports became background to the central enterprise of learning to care for myself, and it was natural that, in those first months of my mother's travels, my main scholastic focus became Coach Piazza's chef's course and my principal reading material became *"The New York Times"* *Cookbook.*

Near the end of the term, I was working in our school kitchen with the other halfbacks, folding beaten egg whites into a pot, when someone at the adjacent stove started laughing. I turned to look at him, dropped my spoon, grabbed at it and caught flame from the burner instead. My left hand was scorched.

Coach Piazza led me to the sink, ran cold water over my hand, and said, "Skloot, you're as injury-prone in the kitchen as you are on the football field."

I returned home that afternoon with my hand in a bandage that began exactly where the earlier cast had ended at the base of my thumb. My mother looked at me, shook her head, and turned away.

"Now," she said, sitting at the dining table, "maybe you'll stop messing around in the kitchen."

But I didn't. I just got better at cleaning up after myself. I learned to open the windows and air out the apartment, to plunge into the oven with gloves and cleaning products, to use warm water against oil splatters. I developed a rhythm, alternating between months when my mother was gone and I was free, and months when she was home and I was under house rules. I learned to look forward, to anticipate and plan, savoring in advance what I might produce on my own.

From the age of fifteen onward, kitchens were at the center of my idea of home. The cookbook from my cousin Emily is now covered in sauce stains and oil splatters, its binding broken, its paper cover missing, but it's in the center of the bookcase devoted to cookbooks. I do most of the meal preparation in the life I share with Beverly, combining and concocting as we talk about our day or listen to the news or sing golden oldies.

I believe that the winter and spring of 1963 marked a dynamic shift of faith for me, the moment when I began to rely on myself, to take a measure of control over my daily life. To feed myself. Looking back, I can see how rigorously I'd worked to shield myself from the grief and loneliness I felt, inventing rituals that replaced the failed ones imposed on me. In my life at home, there were so many unanswered questions and so much inexplicable behavior, such irrational structure and confusing language, but I had begun to learn about the clarity of recipes and procedures, about creating nourishing things from the place at the imagined center of family life. The place that had not been warm or functional where I came from, until I made it so during the times I was alone.

Part Two

When the Clock Stops

History is a pattern
Of timeless moments.

—T. S. Eliot, "Little Gidding"

6

When the Clock Stops

The first person I knew who had actually written a book was Robert Russell. His memoir, *To Catch an Angel: Adventures in the World I Cannot See*, was published in 1962 and was selected by the Book-of-the-Month Club, included in the Reader's Digest Condensed Books series, and translated into fifteen languages. It was also reprinted in a sixty-cent paperback edition that I still own, festooned with testimonials about this "tough," "brave," "inspiring" blind man.

Russell was chairman of the English Department at Franklin and Marshall College when I arrived as a freshman in the fall of 1965. Each year he was provided with student readers, and before classes began I was sent to meet him by the college's financial aid office. On the way, I stopped at the bookstore to leaf through *To Catch an Angel* and prepare myself to encounter a living writer. I remember the excitement of holding the book, seeing his photo, then closing my eyes and running my fingers around the edges to imagine how he'd felt when it first arrived.

Blinded at the age of five by a splintering croquet mallet, Russell had gone from being, as he wrote, "a citizen of the night," to being a graduate of Yale University and even a varsity wrestler there. Assertive, resourceful, resilient, along the way he had learned to read and to navigate a world of obstacles, managed to survive a wild bull attack, ridden a bicycle, and come to appreciate "the sounds, the smells, the taste and the feel of nature." He went on to complete his doctoral work at Oxford University in England, where he courted and married Elizabeth Shaw, sister of the British actor Robert Shaw, who played the blond assassin in *From Russia with Love*. Russell had been teaching at Franklin and Marshall since 1955.

I was eighteen when we met, and had just spent the summer in bed recovering from my second bout of mononucleosis. Stuck there, I did enough concentrated reading, for the first time in my life, to learn that I needed eyeglasses. The reading had been typically haphazard: Ian Fleming's *The Man with the Golden Gun*, Arthur Hailey's *Hotel*, Bel Kaufman's *Up the Down Staircase*, all sickbed gifts from my aunt Evelyn; a few Hardy Boys novels; Joe Garagiola's *Baseball Is a Funny Game*; Harvey Cox's *The Secular City* and B. F. Skinner's *Walden Two*, both assigned by Franklin and Marshall for freshmen orientation week. The only classics I'd read, as of September 1965, were those required in high school, *Silas Marner*, *Great Expectations*, *The Return of the Native*, *The Mayor of Casterbridge*, *Romeo and Juliet*.

Now, still weak, anxious to impress Russell, barely balanced between awe and fear, I found him, covered in pipe ash, rocking back in his office chair. He instructed me to sit beside his desk, handed over a sheet of paper, and said, "Read this letter to me, would you?"

A few minutes later, I was hired as his reader, a job I held through the next four years. Squeezed into a sidechair between his desk and door, I read student papers aloud to him, pausing so he could type comments. I read personal correspondence and departmental memos, magazine and newspaper articles, galleys of his 1967 novel, *An Act of Loving*. Pacing my words to match his strokes, I read passages from poems or essays as he typed them in braille. After a few months, in those days before audio books were widely available, he occasionally asked me to record novels or extended selections of poetry onto tape for him.

Those recording assignments liberated me from regular working hours, since I no longer had to be in Russell's presence to do my job. Using a vacant storage room near his office as my studio, and operating his enormous reel-to-reel machine, I read works of literature in a way few young, would-be authors get to do. In isolated and timeless periods of reading aloud, I got an education in how language flowed or failed to flow, how breath acted as a hidden punctuation within the rhythm of prose. Vocalizing prose showed me that dialogue could function to establish character and move narrative, that a writer could reproduce the sound and texture of thought in the head, the private music of subjective reality. It forced me to enter into and differentiate characters, to inhabit voice and bring out what is normally silent in the individual encounter with writing. It exposed me to the delicate dynamics of scene construction, enabling me to sense when things went on a little too long, when a moment went awry.

I was reading with my mouth and tongue and throat, not just my eyes and mind, learning that good writing fills the body with its rhythm, moves through the reader with its own vivid tempo. Sometimes I found myself gesticulating, twisting my torso, rising on my toes, shaking my head for emphasis. Fully immersed, I was experiencing stories or poems in the old way, orally, passing them along as a conduit between author and audience.

"Let's try this one," Russell said, handing me a maroon paperback stained by spilled coffee. William Faulkner's *The Sound and the Fury* was about to change my life. Russell stood in his office doorway, smiling encouragement. "Take your time with it."

I remember drifting toward the storage room and stopping outside its door to flip through pages that had no paragraph breaks, or contained blocks of italic print, or looked like notebook entries with no punctuation. *I didn't know which way until I heard the pistol I didn't know where I didn't think he and you running off slipping* The book's cover, bare except for title, author, and coffee stains, gave no hint of what the novel was about.

I'd recently read my first Faulkner work, "A Rose for Emily," the macabre tale of an elderly woman who kept a man's rotting corpse in her bed, his remains discovered by townspeople after her death. What I couldn't forget was the dusty pillow with its indentation of the woman's head holding "a long strand of iron-gray hair," and "the thin acrid pall" in the room, "decked and furnished as for a bridal." Great, I figured, now I have to read a whole book of this stuff out loud, often without stopping to take a breath.

But I soon found myself entering another world altogether. Faulkner's novel of the Compson family's grim implosion—with its four trapped, tormented siblings lost to mental impairment, suicide, sexual confusion and manipulation, class and financial obsession—was even more desperate, dark, and tortured than "A Rose for Emily" had been. It was full of a similar yearning for lost, impossible love, though on a vaster scale, a Southern Gothic tale densely packed with intimate horror. But *The Sound and the Fury* was also deeply interior, with its story's disconnected, overlapping details being released from inside the minds of its characters rather than revealed in an orderly manner by some outside source. And the minds encountered in the novel's first two sections, those of brothers Benjy, who was severely retarded, and Quentin Compson, who was about to commit suicide, were so shattered that their stories, their narrative flow, could only be shattered as well.

I'd never seen anything like Faulkner's way of telling a story, and couldn't approach reading this material aloud as though it were a conventional narrative. By page three, the action was already too broken for the story to make sense in the usual way. Events happening in the present transformed into events happening simultaneously decades in the past, and then into events happening at still another moment in time, with characters appearing in the middle of scenes where they didn't exist.

I needed to slow down and understand how each sentence followed the next before I spoke it. No glossing over a passage, no skipping; I had to comprehend and deliver the language in a way that silent reading sometimes did not require. I read a page, experimenting with pauses and breath and tone, working with accent to accommodate Faulkner's use of dialect, then rewound the tape and tried again. My goal was a smooth presentation for Russell, without the sound of the tape being stopped and started as I struggled with the narrative.

There were voices—a chorus of voices—to distinguish, and levels of feeling to express that were somehow tied to the language of each character. Benjy, for instance, whom critics refer to as an idiot, thought in a way that appeared to be hopelessly fragmented, so his section of the novel proceeded without apparent logic, sense of time, or focus in space. It seemed to lack any narrative development, moving instead in loops of imagery and repeated phrasing, full of discordance, of disarray, like an endlessly swirling kaleidoscope. Getting his jacket snagged on a fence nail as he watched golfers in action didn't simply make Benjy remember an earlier moment in his life when he had gotten snagged and freed by his sister, Caddy, and it didn't shift him back in time, but essentially made the earlier experience happen again, right then. He couldn't remember, he couldn't associate, he just was there in past and present both, living utterly outside of time. This was a remarkable re-creation by Faulkner of what it's like to live without a functional memory system, and it captured the experience of mental limitation, the sense of being where time was no longer real. It was also very hard to read.

But while Benjy's thoughts lacked cohesion, Faulkner's structural principles and the flow of language actually began to make sense. Italics helped signal shifts in time, but weren't always provided, so some shifts occurred without a textual marker. A character's name might signal such shifts instead. Caddy, for example, wasn't in the novel's present action, while a slave named Versh was central to the present action, and thus their appearances allowed a reader to be oriented in time. Benjy was occasionally called by the name he had in early childhood, Maury, thus placing an event at a time before his name changed.

Of course, Faulkner occasionally made these signals unreliable. There was another character named Maury—Benjy's namesake—and two characters named Quentin, one who died in 1910 and another who was alive in the present 1928 setting. There were also two characters named Jason: the father and the eldest son. But context allowed a reader to place the moment and, once grasped, holding onto distinguishing signs was easy enough to manage.

Certain phrases, such as *Caddy smelled like trees,* became vital markers of feeling. Moments of bleak beauty, such as Benjy's confusion of the senses when he's near Caddy, became emotional climaxes for the reader, as this final episode in which Benjy squats in the dark, holding his sister's slipper: *I couldn't see it, but my hands saw it, and I could hear it getting night, and my hands saw the slipper but I couldn't see myself, but my hands could see the slipper, and I squatted there, hearing it getting dark.*

By learning how to give voice to Benjy's section, I learned what it was like to be Benjy as Faulkner had conceived of him. This intimacy with character was a remarkable element, new to me as a reader, and I loved it. It was as though Benjy were inside my own head.

When I reached the novel's second section, the account of Quentin Compson's final day as he prepared to kill himself, I felt more comfortable with the strangeness of Faulkner's process. He wasn't going to make it easy for a reader, but he was going to reward the attention being paid. He was less interested in the story itself, the tale of the Compsons' fall, the loss of wealth and status in the community, the siblings' descent into madness, rebellion, thievery, and mutual emotional savagery, than in what went on in the characters' minds as these events took place. His novel was essentially about consciousness, the mind thinking in language, and Faulkner was striving to remove everything that distracted a reader from immediate access to another human being's consciousness. My reading, I felt, had to do the same thing. Nothing had engaged me quite like this before.

Quentin, anguished by guilt over erotic feelings toward his sister, and by feeling himself a disappointment to his father—who had sold off land to pay for Quentin's Harvard education—was lost in a spiral of self-laceration that expressed itself in language at once flowery and bitter. His section of the novel began in a haunted, stagy, nearly coherent recollection of receiving a watch from his father and listening to the old man's portentous ruminations about time. *I give it to you not that you may remember time, but that you might forget it now and then for a moment and not spend all your breath trying to conquer it.* But as this section, and the June day in 1910 on which it occurred, progressed, Quentin's orderly thoughts tumbled toward incoherence: recollections of loving his sister and grieving when she acted out with men; trying to defend her against the slurs of their parents and older brother, Jason; trying to be the man his father wanted him to be. Those thoughts overwhelmed his present action, the final tasks before he kills himself, until the carefully constructed march of time broke apart, memories and fears and confusions swamping Quentin figuratively as the waters of the river swamped him literally at the end. Pace quickened, punctuation slackened, past and present merged.

The secret to reading Benjy's section was consistency of tone, since he was incapable of change or of understanding. The secret to reading Quentin's was flux, constant and uncontrollable change as his emotions swarmed.

The heart of Quentin's section was the long sequence I'd noticed when first flipping through the novel, page after page of unpunctuated lines that looked like notebook entries and that evoked, breathlessly, the core memories of Quentin's last hours with Caddy. I had to find a way to articulate this writing in order to show which passages were actual scenes and who was speaking in them, and which passages were Quentin's thoughts. I wanted to capture the flow of Faulkner's writing as it created Quentin's chaotic consciousness, how the flow broke into froth and turbulence as it hit the rocks of his obsessions.

This was great practice for serious reading and, eventually, writing. Faulkner's control of prose rhythm, his handling of structural elements, were even more evident when vocalized, when the reader had to enact the sort of textual details and clues that Faulkner's experiments had eliminated.

By the time I read the third section of *The Sound and the Fury*, brother Jason Compson's stream-of-consciousness ramblings laced with jealousy and rage, I knew enough about the events that infuriated him, and about Jason's character, to make sense of his thoughts and actions. Faulkner had prepared his reader, trained his reader. Jason plotting and fulminating, still angry because his dead brother had gotten a chance to attend Harvard nearly two decades earlier, still seeking revenge against a wayward sister who has not been seen for many years, waiting for his chance to have his handicapped brother committed to an institution, felt vividly alive to me. *I'm glad I haven't got the sort of conscience I've got to nurse like a sick puppy all the time.* And the novel's final section, told in a traditional third-person voice from the point of view of the Compson's aging black housekeeper, Dilsey, was as full of by-now-familiar family voices as the Church service which Dilsey attends.

Faulkner still provided few guideposts, remaining committed to keeping the writer's presence out of the way. But the text could be read with an ease that would have been impossible without the intimate connections of the previous three sections, the difficult dialect and subtle gradations of tone familiar, the private references grasped, the behavior of its strange characters understood.

By the time I graduated, I'd recorded all the selections of Victorian writers from *The Norton Anthology of English Literature: Major Authors Edition*, 40 pages of Carlyle, 74 pages of Browning, 100 pages of Tennyson, and 104 pages of Arnold. I recorded three or four more novels, but can only remember one, Hermann Hesse's *Steppenwolf*, probably because reading it aloud drove me nuts.

Like *The Sound and the Fury*, Hesse's novel was non-linear, hallucinatory, held together by the voices of its damaged characters. It was about the mind at its most extreme. But the language—or its translation—failed to suggest the consciousness of believable people. *It did not altogether suit me to have the old gentleman avoid my questions and accusations in the sportive manner, and I looked at him reproachfully.* Faulkner had spoiled me for the fictional re-creation of subjective life. What he required me to do as a reader had exposed the great possibilities for human contact within the acts of writing and reading.

In *To Catch an Angel*, Russell had written about the moment when literature first moved him deeply. He was eighteen, a college freshman, still recovering from the shock of his father's sudden death, when a literature teacher assigned "The Wife of Usher's Well." This Scottish ballad deals with the death at sea of a woman's three sons who, in answer to her wish, miraculously return home for one night. When they must leave in the morning, one of the brothers says farewell to the scullery maid as well as to the mother, and Russell's teacher asked the class why.

"To my surprise," Russell wrote, "I suddenly found myself answering the question." He understood that the servant "symbolized all the comfort and pleasure and security that home had meant" for the brother. He understood, too, "the longing for the familiar pattern of life at home," and connected that longing with what happened in his own life when his father died. "I understood then that this ballad was about people, real people, people who lived and felt as I did."

Something similar happened to me in my storage room studio, alone with the work Russell assigned. At peak moments, I was in the place Jason Compson described to Quentin in *The Sound and the Fury: He said time is dead as long as it is being clicked off by little wheels; only when the clock stops does time come to life.* Great writing, I saw, could do this. It could stop time and thereby make time come to life, transporting the reader, as it must have transported the writer, into another dimension. It could break down the barriers between the writer, the reader, and the characters, as Faulkner's had done. Alone with the tape recorder and text, I began to sense what worked and what didn't in writing, what might be possible, what a writer could aspire to achieve. Those times outside of time, when the clock stopped, have remained present for me through the last forty years.

7

Into a Maelstrom of Fire
On Having a Feeling for Thomas Hardy

D r. Russell's high-pitched voice tells me the same thing it told me thirty-eight years ago: "Thomas Hardy is not a good writer." Knowing what comes next, I nod, though he can't see me. "But he is a great writer."

I have Dr. Russell on speakerphone so I can keep both hands free to take notes, and I feel myself transformed back into the college senior listening to his mentor. I smell his pipe, see the papers scattered around his desk, the long keys and bars of his braille typewriter. His hair flares wildly on the sides, where it's white, and rises to a neat black mound on top, like Egdon Heath in winter. Brows twitch, smile widens, hands settle after brief flight. Then he rocks back in his chair and folds his hands behind his head, elbows jutting and fluttering. Only his closed eyes seem still.

"It's Hardy's struggle to speak, that's what matters. To say what he's trying to say. Not the accomplishment, but the struggle."

As our conversation proceeds, I find it more and more difficult to call him Bob. We'd settled that matter a decade ago, during one of my return visits to the Franklin and Marshall College campus to deliver a reading. It's been Floyd and Bob ever since, but we're talking about Hardy now, and even as I sit in my room 2,350 miles away from him, in the fall of 2006, it feels very much like the fall of 1968.

That was when I began my senior honors project on the novels of Hardy, under Russell's supervision. I'd spent so much time working for him in the English Department offices, being in close contact with him daily, that it wasn't surprising I became an English major. When I took Major British Writers or Intro to Drama from him, then went to read to him, we were sometimes together six hours a day.

As my junior year was ending, he'd said that, during the summer, I should think about a topic for my senior project. He'd be happy to supervise me. I wanted to work with him as well, though that narrowed my options primarily to Victorian writers. So in the fall of 1968, having done little more about the matter than glance through an anthology of Victorian literature, I sat in his office just before classes began and said what I thought he wanted to hear: "Browning," thinking *oh no, not ten months of Browning!* Dr. Russell's brows twitched, a language I knew how to read, so I said "or maybe Arnold." He rocked back and flapped his wings. "Not Tennyson," I said.

"How about Thomas Hardy?"

I'd studied a few of Hardy's gloomy poems in Dr. Russell's class, and seen the massive volume of *Collected Poems* in the bookstore. "You mean all the poetry?"

"I was thinking of the novels. I have a feeling for Hardy, and I think you might too."

I recalled tolerating *The Return of the Native* in high school, and liking *The Mayor of Casterbridge* when I read it for extra credit. But that was four years ago, and I didn't remember much about either book except they both had a bunch of explosive, angry characters storming around the Dorset countryside. I'd seen the film of *Far From the Madding Crowd* the previous fall, though, and Julie Christie was a gorgeous Bathsheba. Okay, since I already knew three Hardy novels, and had heard of two more (*Tess of the D'Urbervilles* and *Jude the Obscure*) in my introduction to Hardy's poetry, I had a good head start on the work. After all, how many novels could Hardy have written?

We agreed on Hardy. Russell told me to draw up a schedule for discussing each novel in sequence, and to return next week to get things rolling. I remember that day very clearly. I walked from the English Department office across campus to the library in a Pennsylvania version of Britishy mist. But passing the brick buildings of the campus core made me feel the familiar sense of being exactly where I belonged, in a setting I loved, doing what I loved. Nothing better than starting a new term, getting new books, plunging into new material. As a twenty-one-year-old who imagined himself a budding writer, I was getting a chance to immerse myself in the work of a master, someone who wrote both poetry and prose, as I hoped to do. My creative future felt very close.

Just a few minutes after clacking across the library's marble floor I'd found the shocking answer to my innocent question. Thomas Hardy had written fourteen novels.

"I remember you struggled with *The Trumpet-Major*," Dr. Russell says, his voice soaring with amusement. "When you said you didn't want to finish it, I suggested that you add *The Dynasts* to your reading list instead."

I remember that too. The thought had terrified me as I sat beside him, midway through my project. Once I'd learned of its existence, I dreaded having to plough through Hardy's three-part epic-drama about the Napoleonic Wars. My arguments were that *The Dynasts* shouldn't be included because it was technically a poem, or poetic drama, not really a novel; because it was written between 1897 and 1907, after Hardy had given up novel-writing; and because he'd already written *The Trumpet-Major*, about the Napoleonic Wars, which I swore I would go back to reading. Besides, *The Dynasts*, with its

297 speaking parts, was longer than all of Hardy's nine-hundred-plus poems combined.

"Why didn't you assign it anyway?"

He chuckles. "Oh my, then you'd have had to read it to me, wouldn't you, and I'd have had to listen to it?"

I did have trouble with *The Trumpet-Major*. It was Hardy's seventh novel, and having read my way through the previous six I could tell it was a half-hearted effort, a job-of-work and little more. The spark of inspiration was missing, and Hardy seemed to be forcing himself to write a book. I didn't have time for this. Besides doing my Hardy project, I was taking four classes, reading for Dr. Russell, acting in the Green Room Theater production of Boris Vian's *The General's Tea Party* in the fall and William Wycherly's *The Country Wife* in the winter, and dating a Lancaster woman I'd met in the theater the year before.

The way it looked to me, Hardy had been going through the motions in *The Trumpet-Major*. Fascinated by his local Napoleonic War history, having begun assembling material for the huge poem he would write two decades later, he saw the chance to put his research to use in a time when the creative impulse was lacking. He used the standard Hardy love story in which a woman must choose between three rival suitors, including a pair of brothers, plopped it down in the Weymouth of 1804–5, then sold the serial rights to *Good Words* magazine, published the book a year later, and moved on. The novel, with its distant narration and uncertain tone, its stock and by-now-familiar romance, bored me. Especially since it followed *The Return of the Native*, which I loved the second time around, and I knew I was in for a rough stretch of reading now with *The Trumpet-Major*, *A Laodicean*, and *Two on a Tower* before getting to a book I would like again, *The Mayor of Casterbridge*.

By having to slog through Hardy's mid-career messes, I was

learning about the consequences when a writer creates primarily by will, without passion or full engagement. Because I had to write about them in-depth, and summarize their plots for Russell before discussing their themes, I couldn't set the novels aside half-read, so it felt like being sentenced to read them. I was also learning about the inconsistency of even the greatest of authors. *Thomas Hardy is not a good writer,* Russell had said to me. *But he is a great writer.* I kept reminding myself of that, writing those two sentences on an index card I used as a bookmark.

My frustration with *The Trumpet-Major* was actually my second crisis during the project. Russell had no idea how deep my despair had been at the very start of my reading, when I encountered Hardy's first novel. If the struggle matters more than the accomplishment, then I was doing fine, because I struggled desperately with *Desperate Remedies.* Reading through the cascade of coincidences that shape Hardy's labyrinthine plot, with its fires and murders and jiltings and confused identities, sorting out the wooden characters with their goofily significant names (Cytherea, Aeneas, three different people called Mrs. Manston), groaning at its Gothic atmospherics, and enduring the lifeless prose juiced with quotations from other writers and with endless authorial intrusions ("A very homely and rustic excursion by steamboat to Lewborne Bay, forms the framework of the next incident.") was making me wonder if I could endure a year of Thomas Hardy after all. Maybe it wasn't too late to reconsider Browning.

There were good lessons in this intimate encounter with Hardy's early struggles. I saw that it can take a beginning writer several books before he finds his way. *Desperate Remedies,* though Hardy's first published novel, was actually the second one he wrote, since *The Poor Man and the Lady* had been widely rejected and eventually set aside, its best bits cannibalized for later work. So confronting the obvious difficulties Hardy was having in deciding what kind of novel he was writing, and what he hoped to sound like, was important even if it was hard to take. There would be two more mediocre novels, *Under the Greenwood Tree* and *A Pair of Blue Eyes*, to get through before everything came together for Hardy in *Far From the Madding Crowd*. As a novelist, Hardy was hardly a natural. Trained as an architect, he tried to master the art of fiction by designing and building a book to specifications deduced from his own reading and from the advice of publishers' readers who'd rejected his early efforts. It took Hardy seven years, from the time he began to compose his failed first effort at a novel, to make a novel that would last.

At the time I began reading his novels, Hardy had been dead for only forty years. That's as long as Carson McCullers has been dead now, or Langston Hughes, or Dorothy Parker. Yet those writers seem much closer to us than Hardy seemed in 1968, contemporary in ways that Hardy never could, even if he'd still been alive.

Part of the reason is that he wrote his novels during the quarter-century between 1870 and 1895, then stopped. So while he lived until 1928, the books I was reading were more distant, the work of the middle third of his life, when he was between thirty and fifty-five. But even young, Hardy had an old man's sensibility: a grumpy, suspicious, abandoned, doom-driven, it-was-better-in-the-old-days view. And he just wasn't writing about a world I recognized. The novels were set largely in the pre-Industrial English countryside of Hardy's childhood, and concerned its clash with vast technological revolution. His only primarily urban novel, *The Hand of Ethelberta*, was a stodgy and unconvincing anomaly, seeming to prove that he had no real grasp of city life. This point was re-emphasized in the London sections of *Desperate Remedies*, *A Laodicean*, *Two on a Tower*, and *The Trumpet-Major*, which lacked the compelling reality of the rural scenes that surrounded them. In fact, whenever there's a London portion of a novel, I came to believe, the novel was doomed, as though Hardy went there when he knew he was already lost. Hardy's great later novels focused with increasingly gruesome overkill on the havoc that modern life plays with the spirit and fate of his rustic, land-based characters.

But for all this remoteness from life as I knew it, there was something about his sensibility, a long-standing, childhood-borne feeling of gloom and radical dislocation, a yearning sadness, that resonated across the years. I felt drawn to Hardy. There was a core of deep pain in him, and though some of it seemed connected with mourning the lost world of rural isolation, with the loss of faith or the bitterness of class divisions, I associated his pain with despondency over love. The novels are all driven by a crazed vision of love as torment. It was a vision I recognized viscerally, having witnessed my parents' mutual harrowing, their volatile misery. When he wrote of Eustacia Vye, in *The Return of the Native*, that "the only way to look queenly without realms or hearts to queen it over is to look as if you had lost them," Hardy could have been describing my mother on any given night. When Michael Henchard, in *The Mayor of Casterbridge*, sold his wife to the highest bidder and hoped never to see her again, he was living out my father's deepest wish. I found their enormous disappointment, thwarted ambitions, and explosive unhappiness enacted throughout Hardy's work. It was clearly a fruitful subject for a writer.

My mother often talked about having chosen the wrong man from among her many suitors. This sort of thing was also everywhere in Hardy's novels. Regardless of setting or narrative surface, the central drama was always a character's efforts to choose among lovers. Sometimes the torment was relatively mild, at least for the protagonist, as in *Under the Greenwood Tree* (1872), when the new village schoolteacher, Fancy Day, must decide among the rustic musician and hauler, Dick Dewy, the wealthy farmer, Frederic Shinar, and stodgy Parson Maybold. No one gets badly hurt as Fancy waffles, though the shame and grief of men's thwarted passion is rendered real. But in *Far From the Madding Crowd* (1874), where a similar trio (sturdy shepherd Gabriel Oak, wealthy farmer William Boldwood, dashing soldier Frank Troy) competes for the ravishing Bathsheba Everdene, the consequences of failure are catastrophic: Boldwood, driven insane, murders Troy, the man who first won her, leaving Oak to settle with Bathsheba in "good fellowship—*camaraderie*," which he called "the only love which is as strong as death—that love which many waters cannot quench, nor the floods drown, beside which the passion usually called by the name is evanescent as stream."

I didn't believe that Hardy believed the business about *camaraderie*, not deep down in his soul. His characters yearned for—needed—the passion that inevitably ravaged their lives. It seemed to be what made them come alive, and what made Hardy's prose achieve its rare moments of genuine poetry. Some of his most astonishing writing occurred in scenes where long-restrained passion got expressed. There was the delicate moment in *Under the Greenwood Tree* when Dick and Fancy rinsed their hands together in a basin. For Dick, it is "the first time in his life that he had touched female fingers," and for Fanny it is a moment of erotic confusion. "Really," she says, "I hardly know which are my own hands and which are yours, they have got so mixed up together." In *Far From the Madding Crowd*, Sargent Troy took Bathsheba to a lushly floored pit in the middle of a tract of "plump and succulent" ferns. There, he demonstrated his virtuosity as a swordsman, cutting and thrusting his weapon around her still form as the sunlight flashed off his blade whistling close to her flesh. "She was enclosed in a firmament of lights and sharp hisses, resembling a sky-full of meteors close at hand." Alone together in an empty granary, Elizabeth Henchard and Donald Farfrae experience a moment of sweet, restrained intimacy in *The Mayor of Casterbridge* when Farfrae, seeing her clothes covered in wheat husks and chaffs, blows them off her. "As Elizabeth neither assented nor dissented, Donald Farfrae inflated his mouth and began blowing back her hair, and her side hair, and her neck, and the crown of her bonnet, and the fur of her victorine, Elizabeth saying 'oh, thank you,' at every puff." Hardy also created memorable moments of passion's flip-side, and these were the moments that most often floored me. There is a scene early in *The Woodlanders* when a secondary character, Marty South, learns that the man she loves is interested in another woman, and she impulsively agrees to an offer she had rejected, cutting off and selling her long hair. It is an instant of poignant sexual grief, and Hardy captures its essence, in writing just shy of melodrama, by showing Marty as she arranges the shorn locks. "Upon the pale scrubbed deal of the coffin-stool table they stretched like waving and ropy weeds over the washed white bed of a stream." And in *Jude the Obscure,* after Jude has been left by his coarse, manipulative wife, Arabella, who plans to emigrate with her father, he finds among the items she has offered for sale a portrait of himself, specially taken and framed for her as a wedding-day present. It is a moment of such sharp clarity that the reader shares Jude's despair over the pain love can cause.

I felt that I knew what Hardy was struggling to say in these and other extraordinary scenes, his heat and heartbreak evident in the rare imagistic eloquence, the ardor of the writing. I also felt that I understood what underlay his sense of love's geometry, how rare it is to find all that we yearn for in one person, how we sometimes cannot want or desire what is good for us, how ideals are useless in the realities of love as it happens in the world.

Hardy, whose novels are often marred by a reliance on coincidence to drive their plots, whose architectural imagination became a liability as he planned and built the rickety structures for his fiction, managed to write brilliant work despite the limitations of his writerly technique. I remember—and so does my college roommate, Louis Hampton—that I often groaned out loud at Hardy's use of overheard conversations, intercepted correspondence, chance meetings and missed meetings, sudden appearances of key characters in unlikely places. Yet the fact that I ended up with Hardy, in this year when Franklin and Marshall College allowed me to devote so much time to a writer and his world, was itself a forceful, Hardy-like confluence of chance, timing, and readiness. He knew my family. He knew what drew me to writing. And I was given him almost as a gift.

I also remember one meeting with Russell, when we were discussing Tess Durbeyfield's sad fate, her abuse at the hands of the Alec D'Urberville, her abandonment by Angel Claire. I tried to explain how much the novel disappointed me, with its heavy-handed heaping of debasement upon Tess, but yet how powerfully it moved me. The climactic scene at Stonehenge, so redolent of human sacrifice, particularly galled me even as it touched me. I stammered, and though he couldn't see my eyes filling with tears, Russell understood what was happening.

"This is it, you know," he said. "This is the struggle to say what you're trying to say."

There is a moment early in *Jude the Obscure* when the young Jude Fawley first sees the city of Christminster. Revealing itself in sundown light after a long day trapped in mist, Christminster strikes the orphaned country lad as a bejeweled vision in which "points of light like the topaz gleamed."

To see this sight, Jude has walked two or three miles from his great-aunt's bakery in the hamlet of Marygreen in gloomy weather. He imagines Christminster as a magical place full of books he yearns to read and scholarship he yearns to join, where his beloved schoolmaster, Mr. Phillotson, has gone to study and improve his position in life. What drives the orphaned Jude is a touching, innocent, utterly absurd fantasy "of becoming a son of the University" and, by doing so, raising himself from his humble backgrounds. It is a glorious dream of education's power, and by the time I read this scene, in the last of Hardy's novels, in the last months of my undergraduate years, I felt myself to be fully there with him.

Hardy underscores Jude's determination by the length of his walk and the obstacles he must overcome simply for a glimpse of the place from twenty miles away. In late afternoon, Jude finds two roofers working on a barn and believes this elevated perspective will allow him to see Christminster. But weather intervenes. After further wanderings, he returns near evening, climbs the ladder, and—alone now—watches the clouds part for him. "The air increased in transparency with the lapse of minutes, till the topaz points showed themselves to be the vanes, windows, wet roof slates, and other shining spots upon the spires, domes, freestone-work, and varied outlines that were faintly revealed."

That brief, faint sighting, and nearly a decade of determined private study, is all that sustains Jude's hopes until his next viewing of Christminster. I was moved by Jude's—and Hardy's—passion for education, the belief in what occurs behind those brick walls, within those brick buildings.

I was not an orphan, but I had been fatherless since the age of fourteen, and yearned to get away from the small apartment where I ended up living with my desperately unhappy mother. There weren't necessarily points of light like the topaz gleaming in Lancaster, Pennsylvania, or on the Franklin and Marshall College campus. In fact, the most noticeable effect was the odor of tobacco from the Hess and Millysack cigar factories nearby. But the place, which I came to with no idea of what I was seeking, took me in at a crucial moment in my life, handed me a mentor, and allowed me to find my life's work. Exactly as the dream of an education, as Jude's dream, was supposed to work, though it didn't for Jude.

Over the last two years, I've read four biographies of Thomas Hardy, starting with Michael Millgate's *Thomas Hardy: A Biography Revisited.* Millgate is returning to Hardy's life after publishing an earlier biography in 1982, and finds Hardy's marriages more complex and significant the second time around. But finds Hardy himself no less elusive as a character. So do Ralph Pite, in *Thomas Hardy: The Guarded Life* (2006) and Claire Tomalin in *Thomas Hardy* (2007). Though Pite centers his biography on Hardy's efforts to hide his true character, and Tomalin centers hers on the marriages, they agree with Millgate on the essential secrecy of Thomas Hardy. He didn't want to be known, except by his work. Which is why Hardy wrote an autobiography filled with distortions and misdirections, *The Life of Thomas Hardy*, which he arranged to have published posthumously, as an official biography, with the name of his second wife, Florence Hardy, provided as author.

When I was first reading Hardy's novels in 1968, Russell didn't want me to read biographical or critical work. A committed advocate of New Criticism, he'd taught me the merit of engaging directly and exclusively with the text. But I cheated a little, finding a used copy of Hardy's thinly disguised autobiography, with its awkward third-person presentation, where I encountered the memorable scene of an author frenzied by creative inspiration. It's 1873, he's thirty-three and writing *Far From the Madding Crowd*, having left London and returned to his childhood home at Bockhampton. Writing this fourth novel, he finally knows what he's doing as a fiction writer, has listened well to critics and friends, has developed his literary landscape, and is working in seclusion from his fiancée in Cornwall and from his London literary connections. He describes writing "sometimes indoors, sometimes out," and occasionally finding himself "without a scrap of paper at the very moment that he felt volumes. In such circumstances he would use large dead leaves, white chips left by the wood-cutters, or pieces of stone or slate that came to hand."

The image of Hardy passed along in biographies is of a cooly withdrawn, calculating, self-controlled man, a maker of carefully crafted fiction and poetry. He handled the misery of his long first marriage by spending his days in the study, working. By ignoring his wife, Emma, as much as possible, not talking, not allowing himself to be upset or blocked from his writing. But it is the Hardy scribbling on dead leaves and wood chips that I carry in my heart, the young writer at the moment when it's all working for him.

Early in Thomas Hardy's ninth novel, *Two on a Tower*, the young astronomer Swithin St. Cleve is studying winter skies through a telescope. The hilltop observatory tower he's using is located on land owned by Viviette, Lady Constantine, and he is there without permission. Soon after she finds him, struck by his beauty and his passion for the heavens, she begins an affair with the beautiful youth. *Two on a Tower* was and remains one of the Hardy novels I like best, despite its many flaws, slightness, and ultimate collapse into melodrama as the pregnant Lady Constantine marries a Bishop after Swithin, who doesn't know of the pregnancy, leaves for travels in the Southern Hemisphere.

There is a memorable scene near the beginning of the novel, when Lady Constantine and Swithin first meet in the tower and speak of what he's doing there. She asks him what he sees as he studies the heavens from her tower, and he reports a catastrophic "cyclone in the sun." Then he invites her to look. She sees the sun, "a whirling mass, in the centre of which the blazing globe seemed to be laid bare to its core. It was a peep into a maelstrom of fire, taking place where nobody had ever been or ever would be." I remember talking about this passage with Russell, seeing in it both a vital image for the sort of love that would develop in the novel, and also for a central theme in Hardy's novels. Love was a maelstrom of fire. So was the soul of many of his most memorable characters: the fiery, unpredictable Eustacia Vye in *The Return of the Native*, the explosive Michael Henchard in *The Mayor of Casterbridge*, the brash, untrustworthy physician Edred Fitzpiers in *The Woodlanders*, to name only three. This was the emotionally essential, strongly resonant Thomas Hardy for me, the writer showing me how to write about my own family life. I also understood, intellectually, that there was another essential Hardy, the one writing about the changing way of life in his country, the broad societal transformation that was altering everything about his characters' lives. My personal taste in literature was being defined, and so was my sense of what material mattered most, what I most wanted to write about.

It is clear that Hardy liked his characters in *Two on a Tower*, and admired Swithin's devotion to astronomy. Hardy was not a writer who always liked his characters. I was aghast at the excessive torment he made Jude Fawley endure, the miserable marriage to Arabella and her abandonment, the failure of his dreams for education, the agonized relationship with his cousin Sue, the suicide of one of their children and murder of the others. By contrast, Swithin and Lady Constantine, at least until the silly ending, get to love and care for one another deeply. I knew that *Jude the Obscure* was a larger, more tragic, more powerful and successful work of fiction, but I responded to *Two on a Tower* with my heart. There was a difference, and I came to realize that Hardy couldn't reconcile his impulse to love with his belief in love's torment. It seemed to me that this inner division—more than his rage over critical reaction to his later and finest novels, more even than his financial independence once those critical reactions made his work sell so widely—was what caused Hardy to stop writing novels at the age of fifty-five.

At the time I was reading *Two on a Tower*, the Apollo astronauts were entering lunar orbit for the first time, preparing for the first moon landing, and Neil Armstrong's giant leap for mankind was only a few months away. We had entered the heavens, and had begun to demystify them. Hardy, I thought, would have loved to know about this, and to have written a love story about a quartet of astronauts in which the one who loves most purely is the one who gets left behind, withering on the lunar landscape.

I'm dreaming it again, a version of the dream I have two or three times a year: wandering the familiar campus of Franklin and Marshall

College, feeling at once deeply at home and completely lost. I am late for class, can't find the right building though I know where it is, don't have the books I need.

I loved my four years there as a student, and have always seen the Hardy project as a kind of capstone. It gave me such a perfect opportunity to engage with a master's work, under the tender, rigorous guidance of a mentor who felt as strongly drawn to the subject as I became.

As it turned out, for every Hardy triumph there was a failure. Seven of his novels are considered enduring successes, and seven range from interesting lesser achievements to outright disasters. There were stark lessons in this for a young man who thought he might want to be a writer. It told me the game must be very hard, if half the work of a great novelist were failures. It told me that even at the peak of talent, dedication, and productivity, a writer could mess up. Each novel was a fresh start, with past performance no guarantee of present accomplishment.

All this was helpful in my own ten-year effort to write a first novel, which wasn't published until I was forty-five. My first book of poems came out two years later and my first book of nonfiction two years after that. I'd written steadily since 1968, the year I read Hardy, and published in magazines, but book publication had to wait for twenty-four years. Hardy was with me the whole time, though, particularly the Hardy who made mistakes, who struggled to say what he felt and knew because what he felt and knew were two different things. The Hardy whose work left me with such a deep feeling of knowing the author despite his efforts to conceal himself.

Bob Russell has told me several times that he was impressed by my Hardy project, that it was something he couldn't imagine himself doing at age twenty-one. I believe I understand what he meant. I look back on my year of reading Hardy as a feat of organization, time management, and industry, not an achievement of scholarship or imagination. It was a job-of-work, but it was also an experience of real intimacy with the struggles of a major artist to learn his craft and to say what he needed to say. I'm glad to have done it, to have read Hardy with such focus then, and to have re-read him again now. I have a feeling for him that has never gone away, and that keeps me returning both to his work and to my own.

8

Echo Lark

I serve two bowls of oatmeal and sit beside my wife. We go through our usual preparations, passing roasted walnut pieces, raisins, and cinnamon back and forth. Beverly adds soy milk to hers. After my first taste, I lean back, smack the table with a fist and grunt, in the eloquent tones of a caveman, GOOOOOD! Used to this breakfast ritual after twelve years of marriage, Beverly no longer looks at me as though I'm a fool. She just nods, and we talk about the day ahead while we eat.

I can date the onset of this behavior precisely. In the summer of 1970, when I was twenty-three, I worked as the baseball counselor at a boys' camp in the Pocono Mountains of Pennsylvania. I lived in a bunk with a dozen boys who were fifteen years old and crazed by lust, aggression, confusion, and Crosby, Stills & Nash. They started each morning, as soon as reveille blew, by blasting "Suite: Judy Blue Eyes" and "Marrakesh Express" on a record player whose speakers were strung through the bunk's rafters, and they started each breakfast with the smacked table and grunted chorus of GOOOOOD! Apparently, their method of showing appreciation for a satisfying hot breakfast has endured in me, their leader and mentor.

The boys had grown up together through their summers at Camp Echo Lark. Wherever each might live during the rest of the year,

Manhattan or Long Island or Yonkers, they spent each July and August as a group in one of the cramped bunks that formed a semi-circle above the lake. Moving steadily toward the senior's honored end-of-the-line location, they'd now reached their final summer as campers.

I was the only newcomer. I was also smaller than all but one of them. On their first afternoon at camp, they invited me to the basketball court for a quick scrimmage. I knew this was a test, a way of finding out something about my athletic ability and toughness by competing against me in a sport that was not my best, not the one I was there to teach. They knew each other so well that they could play as an efficient unit, signaling with their eyes when the time came to take me under the basket for the biggest among them to deliver an elbow to my head. There's still a scar, thirty-five years later, above my right eyebrow. It was a kind of initiation, a hazing, and it implied that their acceptance of me was at least as important for our summer harmony as my acceptance of them.

Besides knowing each other like siblings, they knew the camp's routines so well that I was superfluous to the daily operation. I didn't have to tell them it was time to clean the bunk or to stay inside for the post-lunch rest hour. I didn't have to tell them where to go when it rained, or what to do after taps blew, or that they really ought to mind their manners at our long table in the mess hall. But I did have to move them, somehow, to do what they knew they should. To avoid making their cooperation be about my authority. I would have to reach them, and influence them, in ways that had little to do with command, structure, direction. As with good poetry, I would have to evoke and suggest, not dictate and moralize.

The idea of being a summer camp counselor had come a half-year earlier from my new friend, Bob Randolph. In September 1969, I'd arrived at Southern Illinois University in Carbondale to begin graduate work in literature, teach composition, and study with the Irish poet Thomas Kinsella. Bob, a few years ahead of me, was also a grad student, a poet, a fellow teaching assistant, and interested in studying with Kinsella. Before the month's end, I was eating chilli with Bob and his wife, Barb, staying at their house long after dinner ended to read poems aloud. Bob liked the Black Mountain poets, the Projectivists; I liked traditional formal work, and the Confessional poets. For the first time in my life, I talked about writing as though I were part of it. I might have been little more than an associate-junior-apprentice-neophyte-trial-member of the great association, but my opinions sounded like those of an experienced practitioner.

Bob and I spent autumn afternoons stalking around a friend's farm, shooting arrows at targets pinned to hay bales or taking turns driving his motorcycle over the rough terrain. He taught me to fence, supplying foils and masks, serving simultaneously as opponent and judge. When his foil nicked my chest, he would stand back, remove his mask and declaim *what do I seeeeee?* To which I'd have to admit, *you see a wounded man.* We sent our poems out to magazines and read each other the notes from editors, celebrating an occasional acceptance with glasses of Gallo's Hearty Burgundy. When the editor of the *Carleton Miscellany* took one of Bob's poems and praised its "fine rightness," the phrase became part of our everyday life. *Your sweater has a fine rightness.*

In October, we drove together from Carbondale to a small town named Grand Tower, on the banks of the Mississippi River. I have two photos taken by Barb Randolph that day. One shows me walking on a log perched across a small ravine, balancing with the help of a long oak branch. In the other, I squat on a bluff above the river. These are the last photos ever taken that show me clean-shaven. There's no beard, no mustache, just hideously long sideburns and haphazardly parted hair that hangs down across my brow. I hardly recognize myself.

As 1969 turned into 1970, Bob pointed out that our contracts with the university didn't include summer school classes. It had never occurred to me that I'd have to find something to do during the upcoming summer months, which shows you how worldly I was. The Randolphs were talking about getting away for July and August, avoiding the southern Illinois heat, earning some money. They'd found an announcement about a camp in northeastern Pennsylvania, and were hired right away. Bob would be the archery and fencing counselor, Barb would be the dramatics counselor, and as a married couple they wouldn't have to live in bunks with the kids. They urged me to apply for a job there too. *The place has a fine rightness.* Since many of the camps I'd gone to as a boy were in the Poconos, I knew of Echo Lark and its rivals, and mentioned that to the camp's owner, a man named Ace, who was happy to have me as the baseball counselor. All he wanted was to see a photo before making things official. I sent along the one of me crouched above the Mississippi like a batter waiting in the on-deck circle, and was hired.

In the spring of 1970, I played third base for the English Department's baseball team, preparing myself for the summer ahead. We beat the Athletic Department's team, stirred to break a tie score by our pitcher's sixth inning pep talk, adapted from *Henry V*: "Old men forget; but we'll remember with advantages what feats we do today." I wondered how well Shakespearean military exhortations would galvanize my teenaged campers.

In early May student riots broke out on campus in response to the murder of four students by the National Guard at Kent State University. At Jackson State College eleven days later, two more students were killed, this time by city and Mississippi state police officers. Protests against these murders, and against the war in Vietnam and its escalation into Cambodia, brought the National Guard to

Carbondale, Illinois. I saw university students beaten on the town's main street. Women placed flowers in the barrels of guardsmen's rifles and chanted slogans at them. When I taught my usual Wednesday night class, we were tear-gassed in our room because we constituted a gathering of more than four people, in violation of restrictions that hadn't been meant to ban class meetings. Within a week, the campus was shut down for the remainder of the term.

· I lingered in Carbondale for a month, completing an assignment for Kinsella by compiling an anthology of favorite Irish poems and writing an introduction to it. I considered the comparisons between America's sudden state violence against its citizen protestors and Ireland's long history of it, admiring how Irish poets spoke out on the topic. During late May and early June, with our baseball schedule canceled, I kept my throwing arm loose by playing catch with my Shakespeare-spouting teammate. I also planned the summer's dark reading, packing Doris Lessing's *The Golden Notebook*, by which I intended to gain insight into the female psyche; *A Fable*, the only novel by William Faulkner that I had not yet read; Jean-Paul Sartre's *Nausea*, to sharpen my existentialism; Walker Percy's *The Moviegoer*, a novel I read as an undergraduate religion minor and wanted to re-read as an aspiring fiction writer; a few volumes of Irish poetry borrowed from Kinsella for the summer. Clearly, my reading plans assumed the kind of blissfully undistracted time that a senior counselor's life would never offer. I should have remembered that from my own years as a camper. At least I'd also thought to buy a bound notebook in which to write poems, thinking that my usual method of composing on loose sheets of paper wouldn't be practical.

As June drew to an end, I took a long walk through the campus woods, wondering how it would be when I returned to the Poconos, where so many of my childhood's best memories were centered. The cultural mood was turning from idealistic to cynical before my eyes.

I hoped that world of summer camp I once knew, like so many other idealized places, wouldn't be rendered suddenly absurd.

1970 was the year of music group breakups. The Beatles disbanded. So did the Dave Clark Five, the Monkees, the Turtles, Simon and Garfunkel, Peter, Paul and Mary. Diana Ross left the Supremes, Tommy James left the Shondells, Eric Clapton left Blind Faith, Peter Green left Fleetwood Mac. It wasn't just music: Four pals out together on the river in James Dickey's best-selling novel *Deliverance* had their friendships, lives, and notions of harmony shattered; the tight family in Irwin Shaw's novel *Rich Man, Poor Man* was shattered; Oliver Barrett IV and his beloved Jenny were sundered by leukemia in *Love Story*, the top-grossing film of 1970. The nice, cozy togetherness of friendship in the theater world turned into a back-stabbing free-for-all in the best Broadway musical of the year, *Applause*, starring Lauren Bacall, which I saw during a brief visit home to New York on my way to the Poconos.

The message seemed to be that group harmony—the spirit of the sixties—was finished. The new decade was going to be about solo acts. It was also going to be about hidden messages: black lights revealing phosphorescent communiqués on bedroom walls and in psychedelic posters, songs with lyrics discernible when the record was played backward, tarot cards, Deep Throat imparting secrets to reporters in an underground garage. Through the seventies, disrespect for authority was going to turn into contempt, after Watergate, and then into deep malaise during the Carter administration.

In the summer of 1970, I arrived at Echo Lark as a solo act, seeing myself as the poet honing his craft in the woods of northern Pennsylvania, and seeing my time with the kids as a price to be paid for that. I was all about hidden messages, too: Lessing's feminist fiction, Faulkner's overwrought symbolism, Sartre's existential manifesto, and Percy's quest for authenticity all placed where they could be seen beside my bed. The group leader wanting nothing so much as to be left alone. The man among boys tempted to be a boy again. And when it came to respect for authority, I was hardly a figure to inspire it among my group of kids at Camp Echo Lark. Certainly not at first sight, all five foot four and 148 pounds of me, with a face newly shaven and pale because, before the boys had arrived, the camp's owner had greeted me by saying *shave or leave*. He'd run to his car and returned with my file, the photo of my clean-shaven face stapled to its cover. He held it up for me to study, repeated *shave or leave*, and returned to his car.

So I looked peculiar to the boys and to myself, and did my cause little good by gathering them on the bunk's porch before the summer's first dinner and explaining my rules for their conduct. With a fresh butterfly bandage holding together the seeping wound above my eye, and as instructed by the Head Counselor during our orientation the day before, I told my fifteen-year-old boys about everything from daily housekeeping chores and respecting each other's private property to proper decorum during social events with the girls' camp and silence after lights-out at night.

The speech didn't go over well. I needed to focus on amity instead of authority, and hope one might flow from the other, because these boys were not open to being told what to do. On the baseball field, I could offer instruction for the younger boys, but simply organized afternoon games for the older ones and played alongside them. I refereed their morning basketball games. I went to the lake with them for swimming or boating, to the volleyball court, to a flat acre where we ran relay races. Once a week, we walked to the far fields to meet Bob Randolph for archery instruction, and had the occasional fencing demonstration. They loved when Bob stopped, stood back, removed his mask, and declaimed *what do I seeeeee?* We'd both look at the boys, who would say in chorus, *you see a wounded man.* A couple of them, drawn to fencing, became Bob's protégés, choosing to fence during their free time instead of lay around the bunk listening to "Wooden Ships."

The central concern of each day, despite all the athletics and competitions, was to find ways of seeing the girls from Echo Lark's sister camp, housed on a separate campus beyond the woods. There were socials at the canteen several nights a week, but that wasn't enough for the boys in my bunk. I asked the Head to allow coed hikes through the woods, which I'd lead. He agreed, but warned me not even to blink while I was with them. He also agreed to a weekly coed volleyball meet, which he canceled after watching part of one game. *Too much jumping around*, he said.

After a while, as a sign of gradual acceptance, the boys in my bunk began calling me Wally. They couldn't or wouldn't explain why, saying only that I looked like a Wally. I didn't know if it was an insult or a compliment, but Bob said the name had a fine rightness. After three weeks, one of the boys mentioned that he'd never seen me make a fielding error at third base, a compliment that let me know they were monitoring me closely for false pretenses. I guess my being a Wally, who shut up and just showed them how to play ball, was preferable to my being a Floyd, who yakked about rules at the start of camp.

The days had rigid structure, like sonnets, but allowed for ample variation. After reveille, everyone had to appear on the bunk's porch for the Head to see as he studied the campus from his shack. The boys were endlessly inventive in their means of fooling him. One would stumble out carrying another's sleeping bag with a pillow protruding from the top, and prop it up beside him on the bench. Another would shift positions behind a lineup of bunkmates and pretend to be his own cousin, still asleep inside. Before breakfast, all campers, now dressed and washed, would line up in front of their bunks for group leaders to inspect. Since I was senior group leader, I would walk past all four bunks under my jurisdiction and look at palms, fingernails, faces, saying *how are ya?* till the question became meaningless and, appropriately enough, soon evolved into *how's yer how are ya?* Meals with my boys and their caveman behavior became a wild sort of pleasure, food constantly in motion across the table or into mouths, the noise level astounding. They may have had to eat at specified times and without a choice of menu items, but they occupied their table freely, spontaneously.

There were organized sports activities three times a day, and evening activities that sometimes included trips into nearby towns for coed movies. Boys paired off with girls, broke up, took up with other girls. Nights, after the boys were finally in their beds, I could sometimes hear sobs of heartbreak amid the crude jokes and fake farts.

As a group leader, I spent every third night on duty in the Head's shack. That meant I had to watch the campus to be sure no one left his bunk and no trouble developed. Junior counselors were deployed to sit on bunk porches, one counselor for every two bunks, and at 10:00 I would deliver a sandwich to each of them. These were quiet nights, when I could read or work on my poems. It seems as though I spent the entire summer trying to write a poem about my father's death that was somehow connected to a line from James Joyce's *Ulysses* that referred to "the heaventree of stars hung with humid nightblue fruit." I was finding myself too busy, too tired, or too engaged with my boys and their problems to get much reading or writing done in the bunk. None of the books I'd brought to read could hold my attention.

Except for my on-duty nights, I was off every evening from taps at 9:00 till midnight. I drove to nearby Poyntelle and met the Randolphs at a bar where we'd drink Rolling Rock beer, share an order of steamed clams, throw darts, play pool. Bob and I seldom talked about writing that summer. Poetry had gone underground, where it belonged at that moment in my life, like the winter streams of the Poconos in summer's drought.

The Head picked seven counselors to be on Echo Lark's basketball team for games against counselors from neighboring camps. This was, apparently, a long-standing tradition, weekly competition taken seriously by the Head. I was selected because I'd pass the ball and play defense, things none of the other players would do. Given the limitations of my shooting and rebounding skills, of course, these were the only positive contributions I could make to the team.

Within my bunk, within the structure of my counselor duties, as part of the basketball team, I was happy to be part of Echo Lark's group spirit. I made friends with a fellow counselor named Royce, from England, who played soccer and read Elizabethan poetry. The feeling of satisfaction within a community was something I hadn't thought about before arriving there, and hadn't remembered about my distant summers as a camper, always wanting to win, to lead. A small antidote to what was happening in the larger world, something I'd been missing without knowing it.

During the summer's fourth week, I found one of my boys alone in the woods beyond the archery range. Ron was always moody, but in the last few days, after his mother had appeared on campus during the summer's sole Visiting Weekend, he'd been almost silent. His bunkmates, used to his melancholy swings, left him alone. His good looks, I saw, came from his mother, and I imagined his father as contributing the dark hair and height. Ron and I walked the perimeter of the campus and he told me that his parents' divorce was about to become final. He hadn't wanted to come to camp this summer, wanted to stay home and work. Earn some money and, it became evident, see if he could bring his parents back together. If that failed, he felt he should be at home with her because she was unstable on her own. I'd never been through a divorce, but I told Ron that when my father died, I was fourteen and felt both abandoned and burdened with responsibility for my mother, who had never worked and seemed incapable of functioning on her own. In the silence that followed, I realized that I hadn't said that about myself before, hadn't

quite put together my father's sudden death and my mother's de-
pendence. She had always been so explosive and demanding that
she seemed in complete command, a volatile dictator.

Later that week, as though having passed the summer's midpoint
permitted all pent-up emotion to erupt, another of my boys returned
to the bunk one afternoon, flung open the door, and collapsed on
his bed in tears. Jax was the tallest of the kids, maybe six foot three,
but awkward in his body, the bones apparent, the layers of muscle
and flesh inadequate for what was beneath them. He kept repeating the same thing, *That's it. I'm dead.* I figured this was about another failed romance, but then remembered that Jax didn't have a
girlfriend. When he calmed down enough, he told me that he'd had
a fight with his brother, who was three years younger and living in a
junior bunk. *He killed me. I'm dead.* Jax's humiliation stunned me. As
I tried to calm him, I remembered the moment when power shifted
in my relationship with my older and much larger brother after a
fistfight in our living room. Philip's anger was sudden, convulsive,
and wild, directed outward; mine was quiet, grim, and determined,
directed inward. He was stronger, I was faster, and only our mother's hysteria stopped us. The wounds of that fight still hadn't healed,
something I didn't want to happen for Jax and his brother.

During the fourth week, rehearsals began for the coed senior play.
Barb Randolph wanted to put on *West Side Story* and asked if I thought
the boys in my group would be willing to do a love story and work
hard enough on the dancing and singing. I sure wanted them to; I'd
appeared as A-Rab in a summer camp production of *West Side Story*
in 1962, had continued my college acting work in grad school, where
I performed for student-directors at Southern Illinois University who
were staging plays as part of their degree work. I thought the effort
to prepare *West Side Story* would satisfy my boys' desire to be with
the girls as much as they could, would tap into their long-standing

sense of being a team, would give them a handy emotional outlet, and would be enough fun to overcome any hesitation about being in a love story, dancing, or singing.

They agreed with a minimum of eye rolling and adolescent grunting. Barb was a splendid director, someone the boys respected, and they surprised me by knowing most of the songs, even though they hadn't been sung by Crosby, Stills & Nash. Ron had a fine singing voice and was cast as Tony; Jax played Ice and led the Jets into their rumble with the Sharks. I sat on the bleachers and offered advice when asked by Barb. Ron and I had a long talk about why Tony would feel so positive and upbeat at the play's beginning, when he sang "Something's Coming," though he was no longer part of the Jets and was working at a dead-end job. Sometimes the boys would talk about their roles as they lay on their bunks in the evening, or practice their lines together. I loved seeing them and the production cohere.

But I never got to see the play in performance. At the start of the fifth week, I stopped shaving and began growing back my beard. I thought it was something I had to do, for a number of stupid and selfish reasons. I didn't want to go back to Carbondale without the beard I'd worn there, grown in emulation of Thomas Kinsella, as though the beard was somehow vital to being a poet. My girlfriend back there knew me as a man with a beard and had said she liked it. It was, I felt, essential to how I was known by my colleagues and teachers. And, I think, I wanted to make a statement to Echo Lark's owner, now that things had gone well in my bunk, about what I saw as his egregious misuse of authority. Damn it, my beard had a fine rightness, and it was time to reclaim it.

It only took two days for the Head and then Ace himself to notice. The kids whose hands and face I would examine at every morning's inspection told me my face looked dirty, told me to clean up my act, answered my *how's yer how are ya?* with a saucy *neater than yours.* Ace again said *shave or leave* and so I left.

I still can't believe I did that to my boys, though they said they were proud of me. Stand up to the man! They serenaded me throughout my last dinner there with a chorus of caveman hoots and grunts of BEARD! GOOOOOD! But I've long felt that I abandoned them, that my justifications were essentially bogus. I was teaching them a short-sighted lesson in choosing between my naive, rigid principles and the needs of the group. I'm sure I was easy enough to replace, but I should have been there for the last two weeks, for *West Side Story* and for the last moments of their last summer together as campers.

The road back to Carbondale, Illinois, took me through Carbondale, Pennsylvania, a town of abandoned coal-mining fields that had been replaced by now-abandoned silk mills. I felt dislocated enough to find this symbolic and significant, but I couldn't imagine what it symbolized or signified. I pulled over and wrote a few ideas in my notebook, fancying that I was getting back to my work as a writer. I did realize, sitting in my car across from a ramshackle bar, that my past and present had overlapped in the Poconos, the child who was a camper still active within the young man who'd been a counselor, influencing decisions, spreading satisfaction and frustration, trying to find balance.

The boys had reminded me of the lovely feeling, counter to all that was happening in the world around me, of group harmony, of community solidarity. Now I'd left them, left that, and was going solo, going back to the Midwest to be A Lonely Poet.

As I drove all those miles through Pennsylvania and Ohio and Indiana and Illinois, I kept hearing the same songs over and over: Mungo Jerry's "In the Summertime" and The Kinks's "Lola," Tom Jones's "I Who Have Nothing" and Elvis's "The Wonder of You." Nothing I heard stirred me until, flicking along the dial, I heard Crosby, Stills & Nash singing their now-familiar "You Don't Have to Cry." I pulled over because I did.

Through the end of 1970, I exchanged a few letters with Ron and

Jax, and with Royce, but the connection didn't survive long. When the Randolphs returned from Echo Lark in September, we spent one evening talking about the summer, *West Side Story*, the camp experience, and then let it go. They never spoke about my decision to leave, which is really what growing my beard meant, or about who took over in my bunk for the last two weeks of camp.

It was thirty-five years later, long after we'd fallen out of touch and found each other again by mail, that Bob sent me a short letter. Tucked inside was the photo taken on the day we drove to Grand Tower, and I walked on a log perched across a small ravine, balancing with the help of a long oak branch. I look simultaneously serious and foolish, posed there in apparent isolation beneath a sky filling with thunderclouds, clean shaven, ready to take the next teetering step.

9

Numbers

I t was all in the numbers. The doctor had just said our daughter would be born around September fifteenth. That gave us 7.5 months to get serious.

Everything suddenly seemed expectant to me. A new life was developing. I felt that the future had just been announced, that preparations had to be made, decisions reached, actions taken. The year, 1972, still less than thirty days old, became charged with anticipation.

My then-wife and I had been married for seventeen months. We were both grad students and teaching assistants in the English Department at Southern Illinois University. Living in an old farmhouse at the eastern edge of town and raising Matthew, my wife's son from her first marriage, we'd been a typical academic couple on the slow track toward doctorates and college teaching, for whom the future wouldn't have to start until we completed our studies.

But over the last three months, we'd been considering alternative plans. She was thirty, five years older than me, and felt that if we were going to have a child together, a sibling for Matthew, now was the time. And if now was the time, then we needed to figure out realistically how to make a life for our family, because we were jointly earning about five thousand dollars a year, provided I taught summer school classes. We had two, maybe four years to go, living on five grand a year, before our degrees would be conferred and we'd look for jobs. Then, with nearly identical areas of professional concentration, we'd compete against each other in a market for teachers that might offer one spot for every five hundred applicants at some remote institution. One of us was likely to end up doing something else, like several of our former colleagues: drive a cab or substitute teach in a high school or wait tables on the night shift. This didn't seem like the best way to support a family of four.

Besides, I already knew that I didn't want to be a college teacher. All I wanted to do was write, and having studied with Kinsella, who for years had combined a career in his country's ministry of finance with his vocation as a poet, I'd come to believe the best way for me to proceed as a writer was in a job that engaged me with the world outside academia.

My Vietnam War draft lottery number was 327, giving us a flexibility we might not have had if I'd been born on a less fortunate date than July 6. Clearly, the time had come for me to enter the real world, to see if I could find someone who would hire a bearded would-be writer with a master's degree in English who had so far published one poem in *Epoch* and another in *Concerning Poetry*, who had taught composition for two years, and whose professional résumé otherwise included parking lot attendant, busboy, camp counselor, produce man in a grocery store, butcher's assistant, short-order cook at an oceanside grill, occasional bill collector for my uncle's factoring firm, and day-laborer for a gardener.

The university's placement office posted lists of recruiters coming to interview prospective employees. I began visiting the office daily, looking for advertisements that might interest me, and noticed that few employers mentioned degrees in English as being a suitable qualification. Business Administration, Accounting, Public Administration, Economics, yes; English, even Liberal Arts, no. Just what my family had warned me about. *Who hires an English major? Study something useful!*

In the first month, I was able to get one ten-minute session with a man from an insurance company who spent most of our time together wondering if the fishing in Crab Orchard Lake was any good. I couldn't help him. None of the other recruiters would even schedule an appointment with me.

Then one morning in early March, I saw an announcement for the Office of the Governor of Illinois in which the requirements didn't exactly rule out English majors. There would be two recruiters on campus from the Governor's Bureau of the Budget. They would meet with the first fifty people who registered and had master's degrees. No academic field was specified. All I can assume is that they never imagined an English major would bother to sign up, that any idiot could tell they wanted people with fiscal backgrounds. Well, I could compute baseball batting averages in my head, convert centigrade to Fahrenheit and reconcile the family checkbook, so I put my name on their list. Candidate number forty-nine. My time slot would be 4:00 on the following Tuesday, after they'd interviewed four dozen other people. I knew I had little hope of getting this job, but figured that going through the process might be instructive.

It never occurred to me that I should go to the library and figure out what a governor actually did or who the current one was. That it might help to know why he needed a budget bureau and what its staff's functions might be. Governors waved from cars, gave speeches, pardoned death row inmates, dug holes at groundbreaking ceremonies. They had meetings. Good enough! I was ready.

By the time the two recruiters greeted me, they were bleary with fatigue. Jackets off, ties loosened, cuffs rolled, they led me into a room and closed the door. One, I remember, put his foot up on a chair, rested his elbow on his knee and his head in his hand, and spoke to me while standing up and looking at the carpet. He said his name was Wes, or maybe Les. The other paced and told me to call him George unless I got to know him better. I sat in the middle of the room, on a hard chair which had been pushed away from the desk, promised myself not to use their names at all, and tried to figure out who I was supposed to watch.

"We wanted to do this one together," George said.

"An English major?" Wes asked, addressing George. "What, memos that rhyme?"

"No," I said, figuring *what the hell*, "memos that people can actually read."

They looked at each other, smiled, nodded, and started to talk to me. I'd expected them to ask why they should hire someone like me, had thought through how to answer that, and was ready for them.

But they surprised me. George said, "So why would someone like you want to work for an outfit like ours?"

After the interview, I drove to our farmhouse and took a shower. We decided to go out for pizza, and talk about what to do next, since I was sure my interview had been a mess and there were so few opportunities showing up at the placement office. Halfway through dinner, Matthew began crying, then screaming, and couldn't be consoled. I wasn't hungry anyway, so I walked outside with him, crossed the street to the railway station and sat down with him by the tracks. We tossed pebbles and talked, and he began to calm down.

"Hey," someone said from behind us. "Nicely done."

It was George, who sat beside me as Wes moved next to Matthew and challenged him to a pebble tossing contest. Both men said they were married. George had a stepson; Wes had a daughter from a former marriage, and an infant son. We talked for a few minutes about the long day they'd had, about living in the state capital of Springfield, the budget bureau's staff. Most of the staff, they said, were from East Coast business schools, Harvard or Penn or the Maxwell School of Public Administration at Syracuse, and the Illinois legislature had been criticizing the governor for not hiring in-state staff. That explained why George and Wes were in Carbondale recruiting from a local university. They told me that the Republican governor, Richard Ogilvie, was involved in a nasty re-election campaign against a populist Democratic candidate named Dan Walker, who had walked the length of the state gathering up votes. Then, getting back to the subject of the day's interviews, they said they could recommend only two people, out of the fifty they'd spoken to, for follow-up interviews in Springfield with the Bureau's senior staff.

I nodded. Okay, so I wouldn't have a career in budget analysis.

George watched my expression and said, "Listen, anyone who can talk sense to a two-year-old can surely talk sense to a governor."

Matthew walked over and pulled my hand. "Go home now," he said.

Later in the month, I received a letter inviting me to Springfield. The Bureau of the Budget would reimburse my expenses and put me up in the State House Inn, across from the capitol building. Drive up from Carbondale on Monday, the letter advised, and be at the office by 9:00 on Tuesday morning.

I still felt little hope of getting this job. Probably my invitation was a lark, a way for George and Wes to suggest that they'd found few genuine prospects during their day on an in-state campus. But I wanted to follow through on the interview process.

I got out my one suit, which I hadn't worn since beginning grad school more than two years earlier, and tried it on. It was a souvenir of my travels through Europe during the summer of 1969, purchased in London during the Beatles' waning psychedelic phase and looking like something from the cover of their 1969 *Yellow Submarine* album. The suit had been stylish that year, a mustard-yellow-and-brown check with oddly tapered lapels that looked serrated, and I had my doubts about how management at the Illinois Bureau of the

Budget might respond to it. Especially worn in conjunction with the fuchsia shirt and paisley tie that always completed the outfit. But it was all I had, and we weren't about to buy a new suit for such a long-shot interview. The pants were spotted on one thigh with, I thought, olive oil and red wine vinegar from a dinner in Rome the night Neil Armstrong walked on the moon. But the jacket was fine. So I took the pants to the dry cleaner, got a haircut, trimmed my beard, and set about preparing myself for the upcoming ordeal.

The budget director, John McCarter, had sent along a packet of information. *Prospective candidates should familiarize themselves with the enclosed documents prior to their interviews.* Documents! I was already out of my league. But wait, wasn't "prospective" and "candidates" redundant in that sentence?

I learned that "The Governor of Illinois is the chief executive for the state and is responsible for the administration of most areas of the Executive Branch of Government." Oh. "His Bureau of the Budget offers the Governor the professional budgeting and fiscal analysis tools he needs to manage State Government." An analyst's job was to review state agency requests for funds and advise the governor on the allocation of resources to agency programs. Sounded to me like a subplot from a Charles Dickens novel, but I decided not to mention that observation during the interviews. In fact, I decided not to mention books at all, if I could help it. No casual references to authors, no discussion of themes, no quotations. Though it might be tempting, at some point, to demonstrate the connection between literature and budget analysis by referring to this observation from *David Copperfield*: "Annual income twenty pounds, annual expenditure nineteen six, result happiness. Annual income twenty pounds, annual expenditure twenty pound ought and six, result misery."

For the three-and-a-half-hour drive to Springfield, I wore my turquoise suede jeans, a faded burgundy SIU sweatshirt, and black high-top sneakers, and tried not to worry about how I'd answer any technical

budgeting questions. My mantra had become *Don't pretend to know.*
Though I now had a vague idea of what the executive structure of
Illinois government was, the size of the state budget, and which
agencies got the most money, I knew almost nothing about how
funding decisions were made at that level, or what a budget analyst
might do while sitting at his desk every day. Better to play to any
strengths I thought I might have—facility with language, imagination, a new perspective—and hope that they didn't sound like weak-
nesses to my interviewers.

I turned on the radio. It seemed as though every station in southern Illinois was continuously playing Don McLean's "American Pie."
But as I entered Sangamon County, where Springfield is located, the
local station broadcast Elvis singing "I Just Can't Help Believing." The
title and timing seemed so absurdly fortuitous that I had to laugh.
Just believe, Floyd. It was a sign from The King!

That night, I had the standard, predictable, showing-up-naked-at-a-
meeting dream. Walked into the White House for my meeting with
the president, saw Richard Nixon heading my way with his hand
outstretched. He suddenly stopped and pointed at me, leaning over
to talk with his sidekicks, Haldeman and Ehrlichman. That's when
I realized I wasn't wearing any clothes. A helicopter gunship approached, the rotor noise deafening as it hovered, and I knew it was
about to fire a missile at me.

After my shower the next morning, I discovered what I must already have known: I'd forgotten to pack my suit pants. From my
room at the State House Inn, I could picture them hanging in the
bedroom closet at home, concealed in their own separate plastic bag
from the dry cleaners. Had I simply not noticed them when packing because they were next to my jacket instead of hung inside it as
usual? Or had I forgotten them on purpose to sabotage any chance
to succeed in this alien world of public finance? Either way, I was

about to show up garbed as a Republican's worst nightmare. So much for Elvis and his sign.

I sat down on the bed and thought about my options. I could try to buy a new suit, but realized that no clothing store would be open early enough. I could ask if the hotel had a wheelchair I could borrow, and use a blanket from the bed as a lap robe. I could cancel the interview and drive home. Or I could wear my turquoise jeans with my mustard-yellow-and-brown checked suit jacket, fuchsia shirt, and paisley tie, and show up for the interviews looking so outlandish that even if I weren't totally unqualified for the job, they'd never hire me.

Let it be. I wore what I had with me, and decided not to apologize. Not even to mention my packing error or my clothes while I was also not mentioning books or authors or themes and not quoting from great literature. And not mentioning that I was a Democrat. I'd wing it. At this point, I had absolutely nothing to lose.

What struck me about entering the capitol building was how much noise my footsteps made on the marble floors. I wanted to be invisible, but here I was making a racket as I headed toward the rotunda and turned left to the director's office. A dozen other candidates clustered in his waiting room. They wore quiet suits, taciturn white or light blue button-down shirts, soft solid-colored ties, and stood whispering together as I walked into the room in a clamor of clashing colors and racketing heel-tips.

Throughout the morning, we shuttled from room to room, each candidate meeting with a senior staff member for thirty minutes, performing a neatly coordinated minuet that required us to pass one another in the rotunda as we changed places. Our hands were shaken and interview room doors closed behind us with echoing thuds. The interviews were intense and focused, but friendly enough.

Crime is up in the six counties around Chicago. Would you advise the Governor to expand Stateville Prison at a cost of ten million dollars, or spend the ten million on improved education?

State revenues have fallen short of expectations. Would you recommend that the Governor raise tuition at all the universities, or close one university and keep tuition at last year's level?

Sometimes I had to answer questions orally, and I remember being asked twice to explain what's meant by the phrase *Time is Money*, and to say whether I believed that was true. Some interviewers gave me twenty minutes to write my analysis of a problem in the form of a memorandum to the governor. One interviewer, noticing that I'd played baseball in college, wanted to talk about what my position was and whether I could hit a curve ball; another wanted to talk about the pros and cons of raising taxes, especially during an election year; a third, who clearly saw no use for an English major, listened to a high school basketball tournament and asked, simply, "What other jobs have you applied for?"

I went to lunch with a group that included Robert Taft, later a two-term governor of Ohio, and John Cotton, who was the Bureau's deputy director after having once been a physicist. By this point, I'd seen where *why should we hire you?* came together with *why do you want to work here?*, and tried to explain myself while everyone ate their French dip sandwiches.

They should hire me because I could write. Not fancy, not flowery, as they assumed poets might write, but concise and accurate prose. They should hire me because I was trained to analyze and communicate my findings, which is what they were after in an analyst, and though my subject may have been works of literature, my approach was organized to untangle complexity and find clarity. They should hire me because state agency directors, to convince me of anything, would have to stop using technical jargon and be clear, lucid. And I could help them do that. Taking a risk, mentioning a work of literature, I said that if I could read and decode T. S. Eliot, I should be able to read and decode proposed legislation, and write about it.

I wanted to work there because I wanted to be engaged with the world beyond academia. And outside myself. Because I was not drawn to teach literature or writing, but to do something practical with my training, and to broaden my experience. Because my perspective would be fresh to them, and their requirements would be a fresh challenge to me. Because my mentor had worked in public finance and shown me the possibilities for balancing a life of fact with a life of imagination. I wanted to break away from the path I was on: I'd analyzed my family's budgetary requirements, forecast our future revenues as teachers in an overcrowded marketplace, and recommended to myself that I get a job outside my field if I wanted to make a living. No, I didn't know how to do regression analysis, but how often was that technique really used to sort out policy problems?

In John Cotton's office afterward, I saw a copy of *The Hobbit* on his desk, and thought *It's a trap! Don't say anything about Tolkein or Frodo, or he'll think all you care about is literature. He'll think your memos will be written in iambic pentameter.*

But he wouldn't let me get away with that. After we talked about the history of the Bureau, which was still only three years old, he pointed at the book that lay between and said, "What did you think of it?"

"Never read it."

He looked away from me, gazing for a moment at the trimmed grass of the capitol lawn. Then he leaned back in his chair, put his arms behind his head, turned toward me, shook his head and started to laugh.

We moved to Springfield in June. I'd been offered a three-month trial appointment, at a junior analyst's salary, with the promise that during the first week in September John McCarter would sit down with me and we'd decide whether to continue together.

When I told the chairman of the English Department that I was leaving, he warned me that I'd hate the new job, that we'd dislike being in Springfield, that he couldn't hold our places as teachers or grad students open if we wanted to come back in September. For reasons that defied rational explanation, I was confident that wouldn't happen. I'd convinced myself, with my own rhetoric, even more fully than I'd convinced the Bureau of the Budget, that I belonged among them. They might be hiring me on a trial basis, but I was going to work for them thinking *permanent*.

We bought a house on the northern edge of Springfield. I was sent two polka-dot polyester suits that my uncle Saul no longer wore, supplemented them by buying a black pinstriped suit, some shirts and ties, a pair of shoes. We signed up for Lamaze training classes. I was planning to be in Springfield still, come the September fifteenth due date.

I was assigned to the Bureau's education unit and would start by working on a small team analyzing the programs and budget of the Superintendent of Public Instruction. Elementary and high school education was the costliest item in the state budget, and the governor had appointed a task force to recommend changes in how it was financed. I was staff to that task force; in this pre-computer era, my first assignment was to gather, organize, and analyze information about property tax rates and assessed values in each of Illinois's 102 counties.

I drew up an enormous chart and brought it home with me after work, spreading the thing on our living room floor, entering numbers, making calculations. It reminded me of my childhood games of dice baseball, played on my bedroom floor, and the endless statistical information I kept about each player's performance. At the same time I was working on my assignment, my wife was assembling a quilt for our daughter-to-be, making calculations beside me as she planned her design.

Some days, I would sit down with Vern Shontz, an elderly man in the office across the hall from mine, and talk about the history of property tax rates and assessed values as they affected school finance. Whenever I approached, he would cap his pen and lay it carefully across his desk blotter, then crook a finger at me and point to the chair beside his desk.

"You need any numbers?" Vern would ask solemnly. Then he would open an empty humidor on his desk top and pretend to fish some out for me. "I've got every number you could need in here."

He was, I knew, assuring me that he didn't mind my questions. After a while, I think it even amused him to see me marching across the hall with an expanded sheaf of papers in my hand, confused about what it meant to equalize assessments when assessments were never equal.

"You know what your problem is?" he'd say. "You want this stuff to add up. If it added up, I'd be retired and living in Arizona by now. That's why I've got all these extra numbers here, you know."

By July, I was writing papers on how other states financed pupil transportation programs or on the history of special education funding in Illinois. I was keeping track of two U.S. Supreme Court cases on the subject of state aid to schools. And I was playing center field for the Bureau's softball team in a city league. We'd moved into first place, and the man who had asked me during my interviews what position I played was delighted to have moved from center field to shortstop, where he wanted to play all along. I was also part of a four-man bread-making cooperative at the office, one of us providing the others a week's worth of freshly baked bread every Monday morning.

On the first Monday in September, I walked into John McCarter's office and sat down with a two-page memo outlining why I should be hired on a permanent basis and given a full program analyst's salary. McCarter read the memo in silence, then turned it over and looked at me.

"There's something wrong with this memo, you know."

I was speechless. I'd been sure they'd want me to keep working there. All I could manage was to shake my head.

"By now you should know I like one-page memos." He smiled, stood, and took my hand. "We already did the paperwork, Floyd."

As I left his office, McCarter called me back. "Know what I keep waiting for?"

"An accidental Shakespeare quote in my weekly report?"

"Nah, I keep waiting for you to show up for a meeting in that outfit you wore to the interviews. I was out of the office that day and I've got to see it for myself."

Rebecca was born on September nineteenth. We arrived at the hospital at 11:40 on the night of the eighteenth, but since labor didn't seem too advanced, we decided to borrow a wheelchair and remain just outside the emergency room doors until 12:01 on the nineteenth. Savings: one day's hospital cost.

Rebecca was born shortly after 3:00 that morning. Savings: circumcision fee.

I was clearly thinking as a budget analyst. I felt more and more certain of my work as 1973 began, and I was drafting the school finance task force report. I was meeting regularly with the staff of the Superintendent of Public Instruction to understand and comment on the budget they were proposing for the new fiscal year. And I loved being a father to my infant daughter and four-year-old stepson.

But I wasn't writing anything unrelated to my work at the Bureau. No notes for poems, no lines, no drafts, nothing. I wasn't reading much poetry either. I read David Halberstam's *The Best and the Brightest*, I read Michael Herr's *Dispatches*, and a study of Chicago politics, books my colleagues were talking about, but for the first eighteen months after leaving grad school, I was completely silent as a poet.

In that time, two of the poems I'd written before leaving Carbondale appeared in magazines. I remember receiving a contributor's copy of *Wisconsin Review* and setting it aside for a few weeks, saddened by what it represented: the chasm that seemed to be opening between my creative life and my work life. When I did finally open the issue and read my poem, I saw that the final stanza was missing. It seemed an apt error. More and more, I worried that at twenty-five I was finished as a poet, that I would never find the way to balance the disparate elements of my life and be able to write again. That if I waited much longer, I'd have lost my voice and craft altogether. I felt that I *should* write, and that pressure made writing even more impossible.

When poetry finally came again, in late 1973, it came with a great rush. After the children were in bed, I found myself writing poems about my father at his work in the live poultry market he owned when I was a boy, or about my grandparents encased in their very private world, playing gin rummy and teasing one another. Unlike the poems written before my year-and-a-half silence, these had a voice that sounded recognizably my own. And they felt urgent, especially when I began to write about my own life as a father.

I can remember the moment when feeling that I *should* write became feeling that I *must* write. Over the course of my writing silence, I had gained almost fifty pounds. At five feet four, weighing now nearly two hundred pounds, I'd outgrown my clothes and turned into a dense mass. A colleague who worked for the Bureau of the Budget when I was initially hired but left shortly afterward had returned for a visit and stopped me in the hall. He said nothing, just puffed out his cheeks and drew a large circle in the air. That was the triggering moment for me. I began to diet, and as the accumulated fat dwindled the poems emerged.

For the next five years, I lost my way as a poet yet again. Setting aside an hour or so nightly, and more time on weekend mornings while the children watched cartoons, I approached my writing as a program: it was essential to finish a poem quickly, then to treat it as inventory and see it published, in order to justify the time allocated from my schedule as a budget analyst and father. Soon, the goal became one acceptance per month, a goal I met for fifty-one months before finally realizing the mess I'd made. A few of these early poems of mine were successful, and eventually were included in my first collection, *Music Appreciation*, which was published in 1994. But most of them failed to go deeply enough, to discover what they were really about, to find their right forms rather than be crammed into forms I'd predetermined for them. I published a lot of poised, deft poetry in the 1970s, but even I knew, as the decade went along, that it wasn't enough just to be publishing. I needed to slow down, to treat my art as something integral to my life rather than as separate project that had to earn its place.

Working on my own as a poet, then as a fiction writer and essayist, I had to learn that Time was not Money. That my greatest weakness as a writer was the rush to completion. I had to learn to love doing the work, not finishing the work. It was not, in the end, all in the numbers.

10

Running After My Father

It was Visiting Day in the summer of 1954, and my race was about to begin. I was seven, already a three-year-veteran of Camp Equinunk. Parents visited once during the eight-week season. While my mother, I knew, was still asleep at the Guest Lodge, my father had promised he would come to see the race.

"I WILL SAY 'ON YOUR MARK,'" the head counselor announced through his bullhorn. "I WILL SAY 'GET SET.' THEN I WILL BLOW THIS WHISTLE."

I wasn't listening as he described what came next. I thought I was going to win the race—no one had beaten me since I'd started kindergarten—but I couldn't find my father. I didn't see him in the cluster of parents nearby or among the parents scattered along the race course. I looked everywhere, even in the air above the grownups' heads where I thought I might see his cigar smoke wafting.

I wanted him to watch me run. It was something I'd been looking forward to all summer, because just before leaving for camp I discovered that my father used to be a champion sprinter. I found his racing medal, nestled on its ribbon in a case at the back of his underwear drawer. At first when I discovered it, I thought the case held his extra glass eye because it was the same shape as his eyeboxes. But inside I found a thick round coin with the figure of a runner on one side, my father's name and the year 1925 on the other. He'd kept his medal all these years, so his running must have mattered to him, been a source of pride.

He'd never seen me race. I wanted to win for him, to show him that I had his speed.

Still looking around, I sensed the other kids tensed and crouching. I turned toward the head counselor just as he blew the whistle and the runners took off. So I was behind them, hearing laughter from the sidelines, and as I began to run I was glad my father wasn't there after all, to see me embarrassed.

Then the race became pure craziness, an all-out sprint, the only way I knew how to run. I surged past the others, then past a counselor with his hand outstretched, then past the last of the grownups and their continuing laughter. I dashed beyond the flat part of the field and down toward the lake, unaware that the race was over, that I'd won without knowing where the finish line was.

When I finally stopped and looked back, my father stood where the field crested. He glared at me, arms folded across his chest. I saw smoke rising above his head.

Later that day, visiting fathers played a softball game against the camp's counselors. I found my brother, who was almost fifteen, sitting with his friends on the grass near first base. Philip didn't want me to join him, but did nod once when I waved. I walked behind home plate and found a spot near third base, almost directly opposite Philip, where I could watch the game and play catch with my friends.

As the fourth inning began, I heard someone yell "Hey, batter, don't swallow that stogie," and turned to see my father coming up to pinch hit. I couldn't believe my eyes. There he was, in his customary brown slacks and long-sleeve white shirt, cuff links winking in the sunlight, bat and cigar both pointed directly at the pitcher. At least he wasn't sporting a tie. I gasped when I noticed that he wasn't wearing shoes or socks either.

I'd never seen my father with a bat in his hands. I'd never seen him run or jump or play any game that didn't involve cards. He was not a man who frolicked. He got up before dawn six days a week, drove to his live poultry market near Brooklyn's waterfront, and worked till evening. He came home for dinner, argued with my mother, sat in the living room scanning the newspaper and eating chocolates, then went to bed. He didn't dress down. Even at his market, he wore his fancy slacks, his shirt and tie covered by a long and blood-splattered apron. I'd never seen him barefoot in public, or anywhere other than our apartment. The scene before me could not be more astonishing if he suddenly levitated.

I walked toward home plate, staying close enough to the foul line to see every movement my father made. He didn't swing at the first pitch, a ball, then tapped the plate with his bat and mumbled something that made the catcher laugh. He was all business as the next pitch came in. He swung and then I didn't know what to watch.

The ball dribbled slowly down the third base line, his bat flew out of his hands and clanged against the backstop, and he took off toward first. I expected him to be fast, but I didn't expect his gait to be like a horse's. My father galloped, going airborne as he skipped between steps at top speed.

"Look at that little guy go," someone yelled. Someone else called "giddyap" and then the play was over. He beat the throw by two lengths.

He was barrel-chested and barrel-bellied, he ran the way a Thoroughbred ran, and people couldn't get over it. I looked across the field toward my brother. He stood halfway down the first base line, as I stood halfway down the third base line, and he wasn't laughing either. His right hand was raised to his brow and it looked like he might be covering his eyes.

My brother filled the open doorway of my bunk. At almost eighteen, Philip had grown so large that the sundown light barely found its way past him. He pointed at me, then crooked his finger, walked outside, and waited for me on the porch.

It was halfway through the summer of 1956, and we were at Camp Tomahawk, in central New Hampshire, which was owned by my parents' friend, Red Bogart. Philip was a counselor, living with a group of older kids and seldom paying attention to me. But there he was now, sitting on the bunk's railing, looking toward the lake, gravely serious.

He'd bet Davey Glickman's counselor a week's worth of desserts that I could beat Davey in a race around the outdoor basketball court. Still looking away, Philip said the race would take place tomorrow afternoon, shortly before dinner. Then he turned to look at me, pointed his finger at my chest, and said, "Don't lose."

I believed Phil would rather do without money than seven days of desserts. These were high stakes, and as he walked away I thought, *if I lose, I can give him my desserts.* But that wouldn't work. He needed to eat an extra dessert, a second helping that he'd won. Something to savor while laughing at Davey's counselor.

I knew Davey Glickman was fast. We hadn't raced, but we'd watched each other run here and there, caught glimpses of each other's speed during baseball games. He was the son of the great American sprinter Marty Glickman, who as a kid of eighteen had been on the 1936 U.S. Olympic track team that competed in the Berlin games when the Nazis were in power. Glickman had been prevented from competing because he was a Jew. In the two weeks that followed the games, racing against Olympians throughout Europe, he trounced them. But there was an aura of outrage surrounding Glickman and his story, a sense of unfinished business that still existed, twenty-one years later.

My father had his one medal for winning some interscholastic track meet. Davey's father had run with Jesse Owens, had been one of the best sprinters in the world. The Skloots and Glickmans lived in the same neighborhoods of Brooklyn, but my father was nine years older and they'd never competed against each other. It wouldn't have been much of a match, if they had. As Glickman said in his autobiography, *The Fastest Kid on the Block*, "I won city, state, and national championships while a student at Madison High School in Brooklyn in the early 1930s." Well, my father may have been fast, but Marty Glickman had set the state record of 9.75 seconds in the hundred-yard dash, and went on to prove himself as one of the world's elite.

By the time my brother had placed his bet, Marty Glickman was a famous radio and television sportscaster in New York. I knew his voice and its staccato rhythms, could hear it easily in my mind, accompanied by the tinny drumbeat of high school football marching bands or the background noise of a major league baseball game. It was as familiar as the voice of an uncle.

I wanted to race Davey Glickman. But with my brother's desserts at stake, I felt an unfamiliar pressure about running. And I felt a sense of significance to the race, as though I were somehow running for my father against his rival's son.

Before lunch the next day, I walked to the basketball court to have a look at the race course. When I played basketball there, running back and forth, the thing seemed small, but now I saw it was going to be a long race, maybe four hundred yards to get all the way around the court, not the fifty- or hundred-yard sprint I was used to. All I'd ever done was run full speed, sometimes taking myself right to the edge of balance. It felt that my body was a separate entity when I raced, and that I was just along for the wild ride. So I turned away from the court and walked back to my bunk for Rest Hour, a little ruffled, a little agitated, but not knowing what to do about it.

As I returned to the basketball court for the race, my brother came up behind me and put his hand on my shoulder. I'd always loved walking along next to him, and was waiting for his usual knuckle-rub across my crew cut scalp. But he just stopped me and said "don't lose" again.

I nodded. Then, maybe because of something he saw in my eyes, Phil bent down and kissed me.

I was surprised to see Red Bogart standing at center court. I was also surprised to see so many campers gathered there to watch. I thought they'd all be at their afternoon activities, except for me and Davey. We both walked over to Red, who shook our hands and escorted us to the corner of the court. We had to run around the full perimeter, ending where we began.

When Red blew his whistle, I took off. I reached the first turn and looked back to see Davey far behind. At the second turn, which arrived quickly, he was only just at the first turn. Down the long straightaway, though, something happened. I felt myself slowing down, getting sloppy, almost stumbling as fatigue took hold. I didn't remember feeling that before. As I reached the third and final turn, I could hear everyone screaming and could feel that Davey was right behind me, almost beside me as we headed for the finish.

Without thinking—unable to think—I broke into a gallop. I was airborne between strides, just like my father, and had found a last reserve of speed that was just enough to hold Davey off. I passed the finish line and tumbled head over heels.

I couldn't catch my breath, but could hear a mixture of laughter and chatter as Philip came over to help me up. He was smiling, shaking his head.

"I wish I had that on film," he said.

Red Bogart said, "Your father would be proud of you." But I could imagine my father looming behind Red, glaring, with smoke rising above his head.

Because I saw him so rarely, I was always running after my father when he was at home. As soon as he returned from work, I trailed him to the bedroom, to the bathroom, hoping for stories about his day, telling him stories about mine.

Lefty, the man who ran the chicken plucking machine at my father's market, and was in charge of feeding the live birds, sometimes got in arguments with customers. He tried to convince housewives to buy two smaller pullets instead of one larger capon, or to use an old hen for soup. When they told him there were still a few feathers on the last chicken he'd plucked for them, Lefty said the feathers must have grown back while the customer was going home. He talked to the Jewish customers with an Italian accent, and to the Italian customers with a Yiddish accent, trying, my father said, to keep everyone equally confused. Lefty wasn't the only source of good tales. There was a woman named Mrs. Head who demanded that my father sell her the chicken with the longest neck. A man named Herb Smart came in twice a week, just before closing time, and asked for an extra gizzard with his chicken so he and his twin brother, Art Smart, didn't have to share one. There was a chicken who yelled "Help!" when my father approached its coop, and another who stood near the door as though hoping to be chosen by my father and put out of its misery.

Tales of my days didn't bear the narrative heft or comic surprise of his. He wanted to hear about my test results, my grades on book reports; I liked to tell him about running races or playing ball games. The best laugh I ever got from him followed the story of a race during recess: two kids took off from home plate, sprinting in opposite directions around the bases to see who would get back to home plate first, only to flatten each other in a collision at second base.

I knew my father liked to hear me laugh at his stories. But there were days when he turned on me and said, "Stop following me around. I just walk in the door, you could give me a little peace and quiet."

That meant he'd had a hard day, and I did leave him alone. But then after dinner I'd show up in the living room while he tried to read the paper or eat his chocolates. Sometimes he went to bed before I did, so he could wake up at 3:00 to leave for the market, but most nights we headed for our bedrooms at the same time, and raced to see who got to sleep first.

The only day he didn't work was Sunday. Then my brother and I got up early, and left with my father for a morning full of play. Depending on the season, we might ride horses on the bridle paths of Prospect Park, imagining ourselves racing the Kentucky Derby; or go sledding on the park's hills to see who could make it down the fastest; or we competed in games at Coney Island, especially the mechanical horse race that circumscribed Steeplechase Park. It was always about who's first, who's second, who's last.

Missing two months of Sundays each summer while I was at camp, and one Sunday every month when we solemnly visited the Skloot family plot at Beth David cemetery instead of playing games, I had less than two hundred such playful Sunday mornings with my father between 1952, when he began including me, and 1958, when his legs were shattered in the car accident from which he never fully recovered.

The time with my father raced by.

About six weeks after he died, as 1961 turned into 1962, I had a dream in which my father was seated on the floor of my bedroom closet. As soon as I opened the door, he bolted past me and galloped straight out of the house through the open window. I ran after him, realizing he was headed toward the beach and ocean, running into the moonlit surf. Since he had died in a swimming pool, drowning after a presumed heart attack, I felt it was up to me to save him from this second watery death. I was gaining ground, running faster than I thought possible, and then we both were horses above the waves as I awoke. In the dream's final moment, I understood that I was never going to catch up to my father. For all my speed, which was his speed anyway, this was not a race I could win.

As a teenager, though I remained fast, my speed was no longer extraordinary. Boys grew longer and leaner than I did, and began to train more seriously. They knew how to run. I was still just along for the ride, separate from what my body did when it went all-out.

I didn't know what to do with my speed, was consumed within my body's explosion of effort. On a basketball court, I would often outrun my own dribbling and lose control of the ball. On a baseball or football field, I sometimes overran a ball I was chasing and missed the catch, tumbling as I tried to reverse direction. Running occasionally for the high school track team, I hadn't mastered the use of a sprinter's starting blocks or worked on the shifting form required to compete in a serious hundred-yard dash. I finished dead last in two meets, then became a long-jumper, hoping to utilize my speed as a launching force from the board at the runway's end. In the only film I've ever seen of myself running, I look crazed, my eyes and mouth strained wide, my legs and feet at odd angles, hands like claws.

By the time I was in college, I no longer competed as a runner. I stole home during my first baseball game as a freshman, but then even baseball went away. Speed, once the essence of my physical nature, became memory, became metaphor. I was no longer a runner, but I did everything fast. I became a young man in a hurry to marry, to become a father, to publish my poems and then my prose, to finish cooking dinner so I could do the next thing, to get on with my life rather than to savor—to take possession of—its moments.

At the end of 1976 and into the spring of 1977, when my daughter was five and my stepson nine, we were living in Olympia, Washington. Month after month, the only movie in the downtown theater was *Rocky*.

One scene that moved me far beyond its context in the film was when Rocky began training for his big fight with Apollo Creed. Rocky Balboa, the Italian Stallion, was out of shape, as I, the Jewish Shetland Pony, was out of shape. He stumbled out of bed at four in the morning, cracked five raw eggs into a glass, and drank them in a gulp, just as my father used to do. Rocky, dressed in his gray hooded sweatshirt, wrapped a towel around his neck, then took off on a painful run through the city streets, finally staggering to a stop atop the Philadelphia Art Museum's staircase. By the time he got himself into good enough shape for his final triumphant sprint up those same steps, accompanied by Bill Conti's rapturous song, "Gonna Fly," I was bawling helplessly beside my daughter, who tried to comfort me with pats on the shoulder.

We went home and I immediately changed into sweatpants and hooded sweatshirt. I wrapped a towel around my neck and tucked it under the shirt's collar, put on a beat-up pair of sneakers, and went out for a run. I hadn't jogged or run or done any kind of formal exercise in close to a decade. But I took off at full-speed, of course, and was bent over gasping for breath at the bottom of the hill, barely two hundred yards from home.

It took another five years, and the fatal heart attack of my best friend's father, to get me running again. I put on the same Rocky outfit, thought *pace yourself this time, you idiot*, and took off. I was living in Springfield, Illinois, again, a block from Washington Park, where people always seemed to be jogging its mile-and-a-half loop. By the time I got to the park's entrance, though, I was breathing hard and realized—even as I was thinking about pace—that I was sprinting. I slowed, turned left, and began following the loop, slowing some more as I reached the halfway point, slowing even more as I neared the slight uphill by the carillon, and made it home just beyond the edge of walking.

I ran nearly every day for the next twelve years. I ran in the awful Illinois summer heat, my weight down to 140. I ran in autumn rain, replacing my eyeglasses with new contact lenses so I could see through the downpours. I ran in the harshest Illinois winter, with the wind chill factor at forty below zero and snow over ice underfoot, returning home with my beard and moustache frozen, standing in the foyer till they thawed. Finally, my friend Jim Kaufmann told me that there was a small running track in the basement of the YMCA, and that it made more sense to run there during the worst weather. The space was shadowy and dank as a dungeon, exuding a pungent odor of soil mixed with sweat. Like a gerbil in his cage, I would circle the banked track, 21 laps to the mile, 126 laps each night, waiting for the cold snap to pass, and the coming of spring to liberate me.

For the first ten months, as I worked my way toward a steady forty miles of running every week, I wasn't aware of the road-racing phenomenon. I simply didn't know that five- and ten-kilometer races were regular weekend activities until I noticed a sign on the YMCA bulletin board one frigid February evening. It was a good thing that I hadn't known about racing till I'd built my base of miles, till I'd fallen in love with running long slow distance.

I didn't know if I was fast anymore, or faster than the other runners in my age group. I'd learned to maintain a steady pace, to increase my capacity for distance gradually, to move comfortably and without strain as I ran. I felt as though I were letting go of my father and his early death, running *from* rather than *after* him now, strengthening my heart as I disciplined my body and mind to find the best pace, to hear the hidden cadence.

But I was still my father's son, and I did love to race. Soon I won a few ribbons in local road races, finding myself capable of sustaining a sub-six-minute-mile pace for more than six miles. As the summer of 1983 began, I decided to train for the 1983 Chicago Marathon, which would take place in October. Preparing for an autumn marathon involved running longer and longer distances throughout the summer, working up to a few twenty-milers. In central Illinois, that meant coping with high heat and humidity, so I shifted from evening runs to morning runs, before the weather grew unbearable.

My plan was to run the marathon conservatively. I wouldn't race,

I would just run to finish the full 26.2-mile distance without having to stop. So I trained to run at a much slower pace than in the shorter races, eight minutes per mile instead of six. I worked my way up from forty miles a week to sixty. Once, getting a late start on an eight-mile run before work, I was two miles from home and utterly dehydrated. Wearing nothing but a pair of nylon shorts, I went into a convenience store to ask for water, but couldn't produce the fifty cents demanded by the clerk. I should have forced myself to drink water before leaving home, should have prepared better, thought things through, known that endurance involves preparation beyond simply running more and more miles. I still wasn't fully inhabiting my running body.

But by the time the Chicago Marathon was set to begin, I was feeling strong in ways I'd never imagined possible. The night before, I ate a dinner high in carbohydrates at a Greek restaurant in Chicago, slept well, and showed up for the marathon eager to get going. My father, I thought as the starter counted down, would be amazed at what I was about to do.

He might well have laughed, though, to see me crouch down and then dash away when the gun went off. Forgetting everything I'd planned, forgetting the lesson of my race against Davey Glickman, I established a six-minute-mile pace and maintained it for twenty miles. My training prepared me to run the full marathon in about three and a half hours, and to arrive at the twenty-mile point in two hours and forty minutes. I arrived there in two hours. There were six and a quarter miles to go, and I had nothing left.

Runners have a name for what happens when their bodies can no longer produce sufficient energy for running: hitting the wall. I didn't just hit the wall, I dissolved into it. The remaining six and a quarter miles, a distance I might normally run in less than thirty-eight minutes, took ninety minutes. I achieved my goal of a three-and-a-half-hour marathon, but running it as I did nearly killed me.

I collapsed at the finish line, was rushed to a medical tent aboard a stretcher carried by two energetic volunteers, given two liters of intravenous fluids, and could barely walk for the next three days. I had to climb down stairs backward because of the pain in my thighs.

The metaphors and lessons were clear enough. They weren't new, but this time, finally, they stayed with me. This time I was experienced enough at failure to recognize that unless a race was short, I would need to govern my speed, to make it last. As one of my high school coaches used to say about the lessons of sport—learning to play defense, learning to share the ball with your teammates, learning not to argue with referees—*you'll find that true in life as well.*

I wanted, after all, to be one of life's long-distance runners, not one of its sprinters. An endurance man, incorporating the speed I'd been given but not spending it too soon. As my father did. And endurance running was about extending the time and distance at which I could run fast without burning myself out. It was about sustaining a vision of time and distance that made real sense, about how holding back was an expansion rather than a diminishment of effort. Pace.

Over the next decade, I internalized this lesson. I learned it in my muscles and nerves and blood by running alone in the deep woods, taking myself so far from where running began that I needed an equal strength to get back home again.

Then, at the age of forty-one, I got sick. Disabled by that viral attack on my brain, I've never been able to run again, but with this illness I began the most challenging marathon of my life.

Now sixty, I think I've forgotten what running even feels like. But my dreams tell a different story. I remember—my body remembers—the capacity for speed, and I still yearn for it. Last night I dreamt of running through a fogbank. I couldn't see my feet touch the ground, and then I realized that they weren't. I moved fast on a cushion of air, parting the fog like a breeze, and there was no sense of effort involved. Then this morning, waking up, I vividly recalled gliding one Oregon winter morning along a woodland trail beside a creek, feeling as though I were made of the same clear water moving fluidly under its thin crust of ice. I was soothed rather than tired by the ten-mile riverside romp, as in a dream. So my running is still part of me. It's still important as I learn to live with long-term illness enduringly, fully, but far more slowly than I would have imagined doing anything at all.

Part Three

Travels in Lavender and Light

You approach the centre by its own sweet light.

—Thomas Kinsella, "Phoenix Park"

II

Bewitched, Bothered and Bewildered

There's a new sign on the door of the Memory Impairment Unit. ATTENTION VISITORS! PLEASE SEE NURSE BEFORE ENTERING. So Beverly and I peek into the office and wave at Natalie, who's on the phone. She waves back, covering the mouthpiece as she whispers that my mother has been singing all morning.

Singing is good news. For the last few months, my mother's tattered mental songbook, the only remaining link to her autobiographical self, has been disintegrating. Though she no longer knew who I was, couldn't remember anything about her life or even about the moment that just passed, she'd still been able to sing recognizable bits of songs: a shred of melody from Gershwin's "Embraceable You" after I've hugged her, or "there's a bright something haze on da dee dah" when I mentioned that it was hazy outside. Often her songs seemed like conversational gambits, as when she responded to my comment about a recent snowfall by singing the phrase "when I marry Mister Snow" from the musical *Carousel*. It let us know that her primary ongoing obsession—the hope of another romance, another marriage—still flickered. When she hummed a measure of melody I recognized as Blake and Lawlor's "The Sidewalks of New York," I could place her in front of her parents' apartment building on Central Park West. But lately a lifetime of Broadway show tunes and old standards had been reduced to one or two snatches of a theme, and a dramatic, spoken rendition of "Three Blind Mice." Radio's former Melody Girl of the Air had lost the only mode of expression left to her. Some days she couldn't even hum.

Singing with her here in the nursing home, finding in lyrics the final form of conversation between us, had reminded me that my mother always used song as a means of commentary, even when she was in her prime. Lyric interjections wove their way around normal conversation like the rabbinical discourses of the Talmud, adorning the main text as it unfolded. Now, walking away from the nurse's office, I suddenly see my mother the way she was in 1965, avid to find a new husband after four years as a widow, dating a man of whom she felt ashamed. Martin was handsome, was in his mid-fifties as my mother was, and seemed bright, especially about current events. But he owned and operated a newspaper kiosk on a New York street corner. Consequently, my mother refused to introduce him to any of her friends. Selling newspapers like a little boy! Hands permanently stained with ink! As soon as someone else came along, she told me, Martin would be gone. Meanwhile, she confided to everyone that she was dating a journalist. In the days just before I left for my freshman year of college, she took me to buy some new clothes but made Martin wait outside the store. "On the corner," she told him, "where you belong." Then, as we walked into the store, she began to sing softly, from the score of Snow White, "Someday, my prince will come."

Whenever I visit her now, in this place where people live without memory, my own fragmented memories cascade, their separate droplets forming a deluge. Seeing her familiar face, hearing her familiar voice, I'm inundated by images from the past while she remains marooned in the present moment, disconnected from time, sending out her fading messages. Things she says or songs she sings sometimes make sense to me, though not to her, and I feel an urgent need to capture these last signals of hers, to flesh out the memories that have endured.

I've just passed the sixteenth anniversary of the day I lost control of my own memory. At the same time that I was piecing brain function and memory back together, my mother's brain function and memory were coming apart. For a while, in the mid-1990s, we were about equally faulty. I could empathize with her inability to retain thoughts, her endless lists of things to do, her failure to find those lists or make sense of those she did find. And I grew desperate to correct, if I could, the facts she'd either misremember or forget entirely, especially when they concerned people or events I was able to remember from my childhood. No, my father wasn't a furrier, he was a chicken butcher. But *her* father was a furrier, and he was the one who lived in Manhattan, not Brooklyn, where my father came from.

Over time, my mother became able to speak of the past only in isolated phrases that came out of nowhere and vanished before she could find another that joined them. She could sometimes answer a question about how she felt or what she needed, though the answer might not be accurate. In the last year, even those responses were gone, and she could only sing those somehow-relevant scraps of lyric. *I feel pretty, la lah pretty.* Then "Three Blind Mice."

So we are encouraged to hear that she's singing again. Maybe she's regaining some lost ground. We check to make sure no one is lurking on the other side of the Memory Impairment Unit's doors, punch in the code numbers, and walk down the long hall. No need to check in my mother's room, since she's never there during daylight hours. An aide sees us coming and points toward the west corner of the solarium, my mother's realm.

At ninety-four, her dementia accelerating, she sits still in an armchair and looks off into the distance. Nearly blind from macular degeneration, she is seeing little more than the play of winter light and random blurred shapes, but most likely she is registering nothing of the outside world. A small radio nearby plays light instrumental music and I'm sure she's feeling the flow of notes. She toys with a corner of cheese sandwich, her right hand acting as if on its own to crumble the crust and scatter fluffs of dough across a cracked field of bright orange cheddar. As soon as I see what she's doing, my mother's remembered voice surges deep within my head: *Don't play with your food, you stupid idiot!*

Beverly and I bend over her, kissing the familiar bulging brow, smiling. "Hello, Mother," I say, "it's Floyd. Your son."

"I don't believe it."

"It's true."

"But who are you, then?"

"Floyd."

She shakes her head, knowing no such person.

"And I'm Beverly."

My mother turns to look at her and says, "Hello, dear. Are you here alone?"

We fetch the walker and help her over to a table where we can all sit together. At the table behind us, a woman mumbles and murmurs. She sounds like a wordless infant just beginning to mimic the rhythm and tones of adult conversation, and she's not about to stop.

My mother gazes at Beverly, smiles, and says, "Three blind mice, three blind mice. See how they run, see how they run."

Beverly supplies the tune, so my mother sings the next verse, then stops. She leans forward, arches her brows, and announces with exaggerated drama that the farmer's wife cut off their tails with A CARVING KNIFE! This makes her laugh, and she can barely ask if Beverly has ever seen such a sight in her life. It's clear my mother is, in fact, seeing exactly that sight. It bewitches the hell out of her, and she'd really like to know if Beverly's ever had the same experience. I believe that the exaggerated horror and glorious excess with which the farmer's wife triumphs makes for just the sort of tale that always delighted her. Especially when the tale involved a knife. After all, she was the wife of a chicken butcher, a man she considered crude and inept at the finer things in life, an inferior despite his skill with a knife. And look, there was nothing he could do that she couldn't do: see The Wife wield a knife every bit as well as The Butcher! Or perhaps it's simply that my mother, in the childlike state that dementia has reduced her to, just likes the nursery rhyme.

When Beverly doesn't say whether she's ever seen such a sight in her life, my mother leans back and frowns. Then her expression softens, she looks down, and it's clear that she's lost the thread of any conversation, lost contact. I've seen this happen to her more and more. She has fallen into a crevasse of consciousness where it might be accurate to say she's not just forgotten our presence or our conversation, or who Beverly and I might be, but everything that's ever happened. It's the look of memory and awareness so shattered that they resemble nothing more than absence.

We've learned what to do: Beverly begins to sing a song my mother might remember, and thereby calls her back from the abyss. "Beautiful dreamer, wake unto me," and my mother nods vigorously, opens her eyes wide to focus on Beverly, and joins in with a scat version of the lyrics, "dee dah and dew drops la lah dah doo me."

My mother is so pleased that she turns to me and says "Now, how about you, Sir?"

It's the *Sir* that gets me. Even though I know she doesn't recognize me, doesn't understand that I'm her son, that I'm Floyd, the distance implied by her use of *Sir* stuns me. It would've been better, easier, if she'd said, "Now, how about you?" and left out the *Sir*. Instead, there's a mixture of flirtatiousness and uncertain formality that brings home all over again the simple fact that I am no longer in my mother's mind.

Perhaps that's why the song I choose is so utterly wrong. But I've always wanted to sing like Robert Goulet, and his great number from *Camelot* is the first thing that comes to mind, since I've been practicing it as an exercise in breath and phrasing: "If ever I would leave you." My mother frowns, trying to find a way into the song. The lyrics seem to upset her. I stop after the first verse and go back to where Beverly had brought us, the songs of Stephen F. Foster, to find one of my mother's favorites, "The Old Folks at Home."

This makes her very happy. She accompanies me through the first verse, her volume rising above mine when we sing "that's where the old folks stay." It's tempting to laugh at the resonance of it, as we sing together in the heart of where the old folks are staying. When I continue into the next verse, she stops and stares in my direction, obviously listening as my voice roams up and down the song's wide range, "the whole creation." She reaches out as though I'm a radio whose volume she wants to adjust. "Still longing for the whole plantation, and for the old folks at home."

"Listen to him!" she says, her voice full of delight.

I can hardly believe this. All through childhood, if I dared join her in a song, she would stop and glower. *I'm the singer in this family!* I realize that I've been waiting for her to snap at me all throughout this rendition of "The Old Folks at Home." I've slouched down in my chair, hunched my shoulders, sung so softly I'm surprised she could hear me above her neighbor's ongoing mumbles and murmurs.

As I watch her smiling in my direction, I remember being with her in the living room of our Brooklyn apartment, ready to surprise her with a song. By listening to her, I've learned all the lyrics to one of her favorites, a song she always sang when company was present, and I'm ready to sing it with her now, in front of Loretta and Bob Lasky, who have just finished their whiskeys. My mother plays the introductory chords to "Bewitched, Bothered and Bewildered," and I'm right there with her, a *wild, beguiled child*. But before the song's second phrase is over, she's stopped playing and spun around on the piano bench and smacked me across the face. I can hear music die.

Soon I could only carry a tune if I were out of her hearing. Then, as when I tried out for a musical in junior high school, my voice developed an uncontrollable vibrato, every word trembling as it emerged as though shaken rather than sung. Finally, unable to stay on key or carry a tune no matter how far I was from my mother, I gave up. Instead, I would stand in front of a mirror and lip sync to my favorite crooners, imagining myself entertaining a crowd of girls from a stage on the school football field.

Now, though, after a dozen years of singing along with Beverly's lovely alto, after buying compact discs recorded by everyone from Harry Belafonte to Jerry Vale, I've begun reclaiming My Inner Crooner, and this moment of my mother's delight in it, even if she doesn't realize I'm the singer, brings me great pleasure. But also, given the lyrics, a rush of sadness. I may not be longing for the old plantation, or even for the old apartment of my childhood in Brooklyn or the rented house by the ocean of my adolescence, but I do sense a longing for connection with my mother. For her momentary happiness in the midst of such chaos and loss. I believe, too, that though she has forgotten it, though everything she knew as Home is utterly out of her mind, a part of the self that is my mother is still longing for what Home represents to her. A place where the romance of her favorite songs was possible, at least in her fantasies. Where things made sense and people knew who she was in all her glory: a self-proclaimed aristocrat-turned-chanteuse-turned-vamp, the Siren of West Seventy-second Street. Or perhaps it's just my effort to comprehend the emotion I'm feeling, my projection, and my mother longs for nothing beyond the moment she's in.

"He gets it from you," Beverly says, reflecting my mother's compliment about my singing back where it belongs.

"No dear," she replies, contradiction being the ancient essence of my mother's conversation. "I get it from him."

"Where do you come from?" my mother asks.

"We live in Amity," Beverly says. "It's about an hour and a half away."

"An hour and a half? My, my. And how long does it take for you to get here?"

"An hour and a half," I say in turn.

"But where do you come from?"

"Amity."

"Amity? I think I know people who live in Amity."

"You do, Mother. That's where we live."

"No, that's where my son lives." I can see that she wants to ask who I am, and whether I know her son, but loses that thought before it can be articulated. So she turns toward Beverly, is surprised to see her there, and asks, "Where do you come from, dear?"

Part of my mother's mind seems to know it's forgetting. During this visit, I've noticed that she will sometimes look away in confusion, shake her head, and sing a revised version of the lines from Herman Hupfeld's classic "As Time Goes By." *I can't remember this, a kiss is just a kiss.* It's almost as though her unconscious is at work here, transforming the lyric which commands "You must remember this" into one that confesses memory's failure instead. A heartbreaking theme song, one that emerges from somewhere deep within a dying brain whose mysteries we are still not close to solving. And still yearns for a kiss.

Singing her version of "As Time Goes By" now, my mother misses Beverly's response to the question about where we come from. But she does suddenly notice my wife's gorgeous smile, and in the same astonished tone with which she complimented my singing, says, "You're beautiful to look at!" She leans closer, peers at Beverly, and adds, "And you're *smiling!*"

This openness to delight is so uncharacteristic of my mother that I can't help but respond with matching delight. Where, I wonder, was this part of her when I was four years old? It's tempting to see my mother's access to such pleasure, and her freedom to express it, as a benefit—for her and for me—of her dementia. A positive tradeoff for all she's lost. But I know there's no such compensation taking place. Only a momentary flaring of childlike amazement at something caught and then lost, the flaring of a firefly. It has no staying power and it doesn't offset the confusion of her experience because she can't hold onto it, can't put it together with any other moment. Her amazement and bewilderment are flip sides of the coin of confusion.

My impulse, I see, is to make sense of what's happening within my mother's mind, as I sought to organize the chaos within my own in the aftermath of that viral attack. I'm after narrative coherence. There is no narrative coherence, though, just random bits and pieces. The memories they seem to suggest are my memories, not hers, and the narrative is essentially my own. But as she was from the start, from my first attempts at song through nearly four decades of writing poetry and fiction and essays, my mother is at memory's core, is the tumultuous source and disordering force I must fathom.

I try hard not to watch my mother as a kind of case, to study her from a distance rather than be with her intimately. But my experience over the last sixteen years resonates too richly with hers, and I sometimes have to draw back.

In truth, I realize that drawing back, observing her, recording her moves, is a tactic as old as consciousness for me. She was always risky business. Because of her volatility and violence, her unpredictable temper and imaginative cruelties, I've never stopped being vigilant around my mother. Now, I work to resist the habit of detachment, to enjoy what's left of our time together, to sing with her. The fundamental things.

"How did you get here?"

"We drove, Mother."

"How far is it?"

"Fifty miles." I can see that won't help. "With traffic, it takes about an hour and a half."

"You should drive faster." She shakes her head. "Or start sooner." She closes her eyes. "I can't remember this, la da is la dee dah."

It's time for us to leave. My mother's confusions are intensifying, and so is her irritation. I haven't heard her sing or hum in several minutes. We've begun mentioning that we have to go soon, that we'll be back before long, when suddenly the public address system interrupts. TRACY TO THE FRONT DESK PLEASE. TRACY, FRONT.

"Who's that?" My mother looks around, looks down at her hands, looks up at the ceiling where the speakers are located. "Who said, who is?"

Beverly puts her hand over my mother's hand and says, "It's all right. That was just a page for Tracy."

"Well, when Page gets here, tell her I'm hungry." She removes her hand from underneath Beverly's and places it on top instead. Lowering her voice, speaking confidentially, she adds, "I am hungry, dear, aren't I?"

According to my mother's dietitian and nurse, my mother is eating well again. For a while, she'd been losing track as she chewed, and would spit out her food rather than swallow it. But they've changed to "semi-mechanical, soft-texture" offerings, and now she's eating seventy-four percent of her meals. She's also served snacks, not because she's hungry but because she gets angry if someone else is served food when she's not, demanding "Why don't I have anything!"

This explains the cheese sandwich she was picking apart when we first arrived.

Hungry is our chance. We stand, assure my mother that food is on its way, kiss her good-bye, and head for the door. Before she can protest, she's forgotten we were there.

As we walk back along the hall, I find myself singing the chorus of "Old Folks at Home," stopping myself at the line about all the world being sad and dreary. I return to the earlier verse, the one that brought my mother such delight. For all its lack of political correctness, the yearning for a plantation home in this line, and the yearning I read into my mother's situation, bring me to a stop before I reach the locked door.

This time with my mother has been a perfect reflection of what memory itself feels like when it's compromised. Images rise, triggered by a word or sight or sound, often of their own accord, often without connection. At the same time, images consciously sought prove elusive. There is a feeling of emotional vertigo, an almost hallucinatory sense of being unstable within the rush of consciousness, out of harmony with your own self. Out of time too, as the threads binding past and present have frayed.

My mother, I imagine, still longs for what singing brought her. Attention, a reliable way to be in public and gain praise. An amorous alternative world to the one that badly disappointed her, offering her nothing more glamorous than a chicken butcher for a husband. A way of expressing hope and passion. She may not know she longs for these things, sitting as she does in one place for most of the day, unable to converse or relate. But, I decide, a part of her mind which she can no longer access at will knows what she longs for. Even as her ability to sing waxes and wanes, even if what she longs for is only to chop off the tails of those unwelcome mice, this strikes me as a satisfying twist in the narrative of my mother's demise.

I'm fortunate that, despite the damage done to my brain, I've not lost as much as my mother has lost. I'm able to function a little better, day to day. I'm singing again. I can still build something cohesive from scraps of memory. And now I remember the code that lets me and Beverly walk out of the memory impairment unit.

I reach for her hand. Together, we sing my favorite number from *Pal Joey*, a song that reflects my great good fortune at being with Beverly, at having seen a lot but now feeling like a teenager: "Bewitched, bothered and bewildered."

A few weeks later, when Natalie calls to say that my mother will be performing in a talent show, I find myself filled once again with hope. Surely she won't be singing "Three Blind Mice." Knowing it can't be true, I let myself think again that maybe she's recovering some ground. Maybe she would even recognize me again. That would be a wonder among wonders, a miracle among miracles.

As Beverly and I arrive at the nursing home auditorium, an elderly man is crooning "Red River Valley." I look around, expecting my mother to be up front, demanding to go on NOW, refusing to share the bill. It takes three passes around the room before I'm sure my mother's not there. I find a young aide, who tells me that my mother refused to come to the show, overwhelmed by confusion. "It's too much for her," she says.

As we leave to find my mother, I ask the aide what song my mother had prepared to sing. The answer stuns me with its irony. I can't imagine her singing "I'm Forever Blowing Bubbles." With its refrain that speaks of fortune always hiding, of dreams that faded and died, it seems too revealing of her lifelong disappointments. She never sang it, that I know of, so how has she learned a new song?

We find her in the Memory Impairment Unit's solarium, seated as usual beside the boom box, listening to the old standards. She asks who I am. When I tell her I'm her son, she frowns, then says, "Are you married?"

"Eleven years now." I point to Beverly.

My mother shakes her head. "Can you find me a husband?"

We say she looks beautiful and ask if she wants to sing. "I think I love to sing."

"Then what about this?" I start "I'm Forever Blowing Bubbles," hoping to get her going. At the first sounds of my shaky tenor and the mention of blowing bubbles, her face lights up as though I'm telling a good joke. I sing on, hoping she'll join in. But those hopes, like the bubbles in the song, fade and die as she tries to hum along, then waves her hand.

"Excuse me," she says. "Where do I go?"

"You mean for the show?" I stand and reach for her hand, hardly able to contain my pleasure, hopelessly caught on this roller coaster ride.

She jerks away, closes her eyes, and snarls, "Just tell me where to go."

"Do you have to use the bathroom?"

"No! I have to find a husband. Where do I go to find a husband?"

I haven't heard this level of desperation from my mother since her second husband died a dozen years ago. It strikes me that all her songs of romance and enduring love have now evaporated, leaving behind this pure distillate of yearning.

The visit isn't going the way I'd scripted it. We can't sidetrack her. We say an eligible man would certainly find someone as lovely as she, but that does no good. She stares up at my face for a moment. Then, her voice softening, deepening, she says, "I don't care so much about looks, you know. Why couldn't you be my husband?"

"Because I'm your son."

"But I want a husband, not a son."

I sit again, put my hand on hers, and am silent. There doesn't seem to be any song to sing.

12

The Voice of the Past

The past is never dead. It's not even past.
—William Faulkner, *Requiem for a Nun*

Fact-checkers at the *New York Times Magazine* couldn't confirm my mother's pivotal story. She'd been, she always said, radio's Melody Girl of the Air in the mid-1930s, star of her own show on WBNX in the Bronx. Twenty-something and bound for fame, she was scheduled opposite Rudy Vallee, played the piano and sang, admitted she was better than Ethel Merman or Billie Holiday, was the darling of George Gershwin and Cole Porter.

Wrapped in plastic bags on the top shelf of our hall closet was a short stack of scratchy seventy-eight-rpm records. She said they contained a selection of her best performances, and even though their tremulous soprano sounded nothing like her familiar smoke-shot contralto, I grew up believing her.

But my mother had lost the last link with her own story when she lost the ability to sing, and was way beyond a final reckoning with the Melody Girl of the Air story. After she failed to perform in the talent show, I'd written a brief tribute to her life of song, and now the magazine was seeking verification of every point in my thousand-word essay.

They called Natalie at the Memory Impairment Unit, confirming my mother's presence there and her history of singing at the nursing home. Yes, she'd loved to perform, and would sing or scat rather than talk. Yes, though she'd rehearsed as usual, she declined to appear for her talent show performance, refusing to leave the familiar sanctity of the Unit. And, yes, a male resident did sing "Red River Valley" as part of the program. The fact-checkers determined that there was a strip-tease number in the Rodgers and Hart musical *Pal Joey*, though they grudgingly had to take my word that my mother performed it in the basement of our Brooklyn synagogue in 1955. But the key fact, the one on which the whole tribute turned, was the existence of my mother's radio show, and the *New York Times Magazine* could find no evidence of it. WBNX no longer existed, but at least the fact-checkers verified that it had. Schedules and details of the station's 1930s programming were unavailable.

I maintained that even if it was untrue, even if my mother had lied about this fundamental aspect of her history, it would only underscore the power of her starstruck dreams. In the end, the editors decided to publish my essay despite the potential for factual error regarding the Melody Girl of the Air.

It appeared on a summer Sunday in 2004, and early that morning I received a call from Howard "Pee-Wee" Kahn. A stranger to me, he lived in Boca Raton, was ninety, had read the essay, and was now finished crying.

"I used to drive your mother to the radio station for her shows!"

For most people, the past drifts off into haze, fading as they move toward the future. It's supposed to do that. "We forget because we must / And not because we will," as Matthew Arnold says in "Absence." Our brains would quickly be overloaded if everything that happened to us, everything we thought and felt, everything we saw and heard, remained vividly present. Only certain memories are retained, often the worst or best of our experience, burnt into our brain cells, the intense moments we keep returning to. This filtered, condensed version of our lives, though it can't possibly contain all our experience, is our essential Book of Self, our story.

But for some people, the past vanishes in a flash, explodes, sundered by traumatic brain injury or illness. The Book of Self comes unbound, its pages scattered, shredded, or vaporized. That's what happened to me in December 1988, and though I can now walk without a cane, I still can't maintain balance with my eyes closed, or with my head titled back and arms spread like a man welcoming the sunlight. Beverly and I have lived in our new Portland home more than seven months now, but I routinely lose my way back once I've left the neighborhood. I continue to confuse words, assuring my in-laws that I've brought a *clasp of tea* along on our late-summer trip to *ping fruiteries*, rather than bringing a *flask of tea* as we *pick huckleberries*. I tell my daughter that it's been *wealthy* rather than *lovely* to speak with her on the phone. Which I suppose it has, since I feel richer in love. In a bustling restaurant, I bite my tongue—and need four stitches to close the wound—trying to talk and eat at the same time. When the phone rings while I'm making lunch, I put the receiver down on the countertop as I talk into a paring knife.

But the worst, most disabling damage remains the failure of my memory systems, both long and short term. My most intimate story, my sense of who I was, had been shattered in the aftermath of that attack. I felt severed from myself, abandoned in alien territory. Memory, that familiar voice of the past in my head, went silent after I got sick. No, not silent exactly, but its sound became whispery gibberish, a mixture of occasionally recognizable words or phrases scattered among the nonsense and static. For the last two decades, I've been learning to find and retain the voice.

When I first began to write again, the words, images, lines, and disconnected notes that emerged were filed in various folders: *Brooklyn, Long Beach, Baseball, Summer Camps, Mother, Father, Philip, Franklin and Marshall College.* I had a folder for my daughter, Rebecca, another for Beverly. It was as though, from the very start, I was organizing the fragments of memory into a shape that would eventually become this book, finished twenty years later.

To stimulate recall, I listened to music from various periods in my life, doo-wop and show tunes and Chopin, campfire songs and the British invasion, Buddy Holly, the Weavers. I read out-of-print novels that I'd read before but could barely remember, rented old movies and compilations of television programs, followed the least flickering of recall. Certain that the 1964 movie *Youngblood Hawke* had been important to me as a teenager, but unable to remember why or to locate a video, I read the Herman Wouk novel on which it was based. Partway through, as the title character publishes his first novel, I was overwhelmed with the sense of my seventeen-year-old self crying in the movie theater and thinking that the writing life would be for me. Even if I didn't look like the actor James Franciscus.

At the time I was beginning to do this work, my brother was dying of kidney failure, his own memories compromised by the side effects of dialysis and renal toxicities. Visits to his California apartment would often include long periods of silence, then a word or phrase from one of us might spark a glimmer of memory.

"I remember we used to go out with dad on Sunday mornings," I murmured, sitting on the floor beside his recliner as he rocked. "We'd stop at a diner."

Philip nodded, his blind eyes shut, and said, "Toomey's." Suddenly I could see the diner whole, from its chrome and red leather stools to its sign proclaiming Special Today that had nothing else written on it and its air of sweetness. I could glimpse Toomey himself skewering a customer's bill and slamming his cash drawer shut. I wrote a poem about it.

As I grew more able to piece together the fragments and finish a piece of writing, occasionally a poem or essay I published would find readers who knew me, knew my family, and possessed bits of the story I was seeking to assemble. They found me, and soon I began to hear the voice of the past as something different than I'd thought it was: a chorus, with soloists stepping forward, my own ragged voice growing more audible as it found its way back.

In early 2000, out of cyberspace blue, I received e-mails from Toomey's daughters. "I think your poem is very evocative of the diner as it was," Pat Toomey Noonan wrote. "My father, John, who is the fellow who skewered your bill, died in 1981." I was astounded. Through all the chaos of brain damage, I had remembered that detail correctly, having found it when the mention of a diner sparked my brother's lost memories. "Your images are all true," Peg Toomey Fisk wrote, a few days after her sister. She kept repeating the word *true*, and every time she did I felt like weeping because it was a confirmation that I did still have accurate memories, and that I was developing a way to find them again, even if I couldn't easily put them together. "What rings so true to me is the serenity of the place. It's true; it was bustling, noisy, and reeked of that wonderful spattering grease, but I always felt at home there."

The idea that other people could not only be part of, but could contain my memories, hadn't struck me before. They had sentences, paragraphs, sometimes whole pages of my Book of Self. In a very real sense, this experience of memory loss lifted me out of myself, and made me part of something larger. Not just the community of the sick, but the wider community of selves.

There were letters, one by one, from the family that had lived in the apartment below ours in Brooklyn fifty years ago. The son, a contemporary of my brother, wrote of remembering my mother "at the piano, foot on the pedal, both hands on the keys, rising from the stool for a high note." So I hadn't been exaggerating when I told Beverly about that! The daughter remembered my father as a civil defense warden, wearing a white helmet and herding neighbors into the basement during midnight drills. I relished these sudden irruptions, the feeling that my past was alive and trying to find me, talk to me. That I was finding myself, and my story was beginning to cohere. That I had not lost all my memories, only the connections, the fit.

I received e-mails from three of my brother's early girlfriends, patching together a forgotten picture of him as an unlikely, overweight, teenaged Lothario. A woman from the Bronx, who had met our family at a Catskills summer resort, remembered my brother as "feisty in person as well as body." She also recalled coming to our Brooklyn apartment in order to meet Philip again. "I think he and I would've been good adult friends." This sense of my brother's charm brought me a fresh perspective, something I might never have had without hearing these voices from the past.

An e-mail from Aaron "Red" Bogart, owner of the New Hampshire summer camp I attended in 1956, told me that he'd worked briefly for my father in the chicken market. "He was a hard worker, loved by all the Mafia women who came in to buy from him, and trusted him implicitly." There was no one else alive in my life who remembered my father from that time, except me, and my memories were those of a small child who remembered his father's bloody apron and the cries of terrified chickens as he approached their coops. Red had met my mother before her marriage, coming to visit her brother at the family's fur shop. He found my mother "flirtatious and I guess looking to get married." He also found her unstable, "one tough customer to deal with," and thought she'd been spoiled by her parents. But he also praised my mother's sense of humor and found her "always ready for a good laugh." Now that was news to me, and sad, suggesting that the years after Red knew her—when she married my father and had her two children—had taken away her laughter. Red also remembered my race with Davey Glickman, at which he officiated.

A letter from my childhood friend, Billy Babiskin, whom I hadn't seen in forty years, was addressed in part to my wife and daughter, filling them in on what I was like as a kid. "He could run like the wind," Billy told them. "My dad said Floyd had a rocket up his *toches*." And he remembered me singing "Sonny Boy" in a fund-raising duet with my mother at the synagogue. Not, fortunately, the same one where she performed her striptease.

Within the space of five years, I received letters from the entire group of six adolescent friends who'd lived in my Long Beach neighborhood, and with whom I'd played daily for so many years. Scattered now, they weren't in touch with one another, but had each found me. Larry Salander remembered the night my father died, and a walk we took along the beach during the eye of a hurricane; Johnny Frank remembered our summer jobs together, cooking at a beachfront fast-food grill, or selling snacks on the shore from boxes strapped to our backs; Lester Silverman remembered my brother driving us to Nathan's for hot dogs and custard cones; Jay Shaffer remembered our late-night raid over the walls of the Lido Hotel as well as the entire lineup from our slow-pitch softball team, names that brought back faces and events. Fellow summer campers from my years in the Poconos remembered running races and softball games I thought perhaps I'd imagined, lying in bed or in my recliner as I began the slow process of recovering myself. My folders were filling with vital bits of information, essential links to the things I myself remembered.

By 2004, when Pee-Wee Kahn called to talk about my mother's radio show, I was more delighted than surprised to hear from him, though I had not known of his existence before. Because clearly, as William Faulkner said in his 1951 novel *Requiem for a Nun*, the past wasn't dead at all. In fact, the past was so alive that I'd begun expecting it to find me, to assert itself, as long as I continued making the effort to gather up the fragments. This phenomenon is hardly unique to me, of course; many of us have found our pasts looking for us: an e-mail from a high school classmate, letter from a retired teacher, late-night phone call from a former lover, daughter's early drawing tucked inside the pages of an old chapbook of poems.

After Pee-Wee told me about taking my mother to WBNX for her radio shows, I could hardly wait to send an e-mail to the *New York Times Magazine* fact-checkers. But then, when I asked how he'd come to know my mother, Pee-Wee said that he was a friend of her brother, Barney. My mother's brother was named Al, not Barney. Maybe at ninety Pee-Wee had his facts confused, maybe it wasn't my mother he drove to the station.

"Barney?"

"That's what we called Al, because with those eyes he looked like Barney Google from the comics."

"How well did you know him?"

"We met at summer camp. I'm telling you, we were like brothers. I'd stay over at their apartment three times a week."

Soon, Pee-Wee was telling me all about the Melody Girl of the Air. It was, he thought, a fifteen-minute show. Songs, and a little sitcom skit. My mother and her brother would work on the script as Pee-Wee drove them from Manhattan to the Bronx. "She'd play a few chords and sing a song or two, do this little comedy bit with the producer as her partner, then sing another song, and good-bye." He chuckled, coughed to clear his gnarled, knobby voice. "Your mother kept trying to convince Barney to come on the air with her. Take part in a skit."

"Did he ever?"

"Are you kidding? We'd go have a cup of coffee and pick her up after. But she'd nag her parents to make Barney do it."

The show, Pee-Wee thought, ran for a few months. The producer, another friend whose name really was Barney, got fired, and my mother's career was over.

"What was she like when she was in her twenties?"

Pee-Wee took a long breath. "Delusions of grandeur," he said. Then, after a clearing his throat, he added, "Uppity, you might say. Let's put it this way. No man was good enough for the Melody Girl." For a moment, I wondered if this was the talk of a rejected swain. He seemed wistful, hurt, as if he'd taken her attitude personally. Had my mother's hifalutin ways broken hearts other than her own?

When I think of the voice of the past, I think of Pee-Wee's thick bass, the way it sounds swamped by all the years that have gone by, the way it seems to rise from somewhere down below me. I also think of the clear, mellow soprano of Alice Sachs, who returned to my life in 2004 after an absence of fifty-two years. Her familiar snowy voice seems to drift down over me.

In early February, I received a letter from Alice, who had recently moved to the Portland area and seen an article in the newspaper about my work. "Many, many, MANY years ago in Brooklyn," she wrote, "I knew a Skloot family—Lillian, Harry, Floyd, and Philip and her brother Barney." In the early 1950s, Alice had been married to the obstetrician who delivered me. Her husband had been part of the summer camp group, along with his cousin Red Bogart, Pee-Wee Kahn, and my uncle. It seemed so unlikely and so generous that these elderly people—scattered in New Hampshire, Florida, Oregon—all knew one another, all knew me and my family, all had lost touch, but had each independently come upon my writing and bothered to track me down.

Alice remembered my family vividly. "We were not close," she wrote, but "I remember how they looked and I remember, clearly, the apartment they lived in." And, as I soon discovered, she also remembered my mother so well that she could do a harrowingly accurate impersonation. A former actress and musician, a practicing psychologist, Alice captured the tilt of my mother's head, her pursed lips and widened eyes as she spoke in her faux continental accent.

She enacted the familiar scene in which my mother would seek to charm her guests with talk of the theater or music, then suddenly stop and turn her head to shriek at my father *Harry, shut your mouth when I'm talking!* then turn back to resume her hostess voice as if no interruption had occurred.

"Some friendships have a short shelf-life," she wrote. After her divorce, she lost touch with her husband's friends and never saw my family again. But now here was the Skloot name. I was a part of her memory as she was a part of mine, and we'd found each other again, jabbering of the past on the phone and then during dinner visits. Alice attended a reading I gave at Portland State University, and I loved hearing her laugh when I read about my mother's performance of the striptease number from *Pal Joey*. She remembered the event, too. She had also been at my brother's Bar Mitzvah in 1952. I found a photograph of her in the album commemorating that event, and showed it to her when she came to dinner.

Beverly and I are driving south on Interstate 5, listening to a compilation of unreleased Crosby, Stills, Nash & Young music. There are studio out-takes and sketchy experiments, alternate versions of familiar hits, songs that were never released, gorgeous guitar riffs, chatter. We're singing along, reminiscing about where we were when we last heard this number, laughing as we head toward home.

The CD arrived in the mail from one of the fifteen-year-old boys, now fifty-two, who had been in my bunk when I was a counselor at Camp Echo Lark during the summer of 1970. He'd seen my essay about it in *Colorado Review*.

When "Everybody's Talkin'" comes on, a song I didn't know Crosby, Stills, Nash & Young had ever recorded, I'm flooded with associations. Their distinctive harmonies put me back in the summer mountain air of Pennsylvania, playing baseball on the hard-packed infield dirt, and the song itself brings to mind the 1969 movie *Midnight Cowboy*, for which Harry Nilsson recorded it. I remember a moment I hadn't thought about in four decades, shortly after graduation from college and before the start of grad school, when I traveled in Europe and tried to supplement my savings by singing "Everybody's Talkin'" on a Copenhagen street corner.

When we get home, I make notes about that summer trip, and then get an e-mail from someone who had acted in a college production of *Measure for Measure* with me, and remembered my "irreverence" as Pompey the Bawd. This triggers a memory of trying and failing to recall that character's long jailhouse speech as I walked in the dense woods surrounding the house where Beverly and I lived for fourteen years.

It feels as if the past is all around me, whether I remember it or not. This has become a deeply familiar sensation over the last decade. As the British biographer and memoirist Michael Holroyd has written, "We live in a forest of family trees, and the branches reach out in complicated paths over unexpectedly long distances." I'm so deeply connected to so many people, my past alive in theirs, yet only now, as I've worked to restore the fragments of my damaged memory, have I become aware of the ongoing flow between and among us, like swirling wind through the oak, fir, and maple trees around our house that I have left behind but still inhabit in dreams.

13

Shine On

When Beverly and I enter the nursing home, its doors always close behind us with a sigh. I know it's a good sound indicating regular maintenance and a firm seal against the weather. A facility in superb condition. But I hear it as a muffled gulp all around me, like being swallowed.

We sign in at the front desk, where the phone rings with a soft chirp and the receptionist whispers a greeting. As usual, a man named Clarence sits in his wheelchair before a bin of cookies, chewing solemnly. A middle-aged man wearing a wrinkled linen jacket stands beside his mother, patting her shoulder as she nods in sleep. We put on Visitor tags and approach the locked doors of the Memory Impairment Unit.

As soon as we enter the unit, we're swamped by a woman's high-pitched shrieks. "HELP ME! SOMEBODY HELP ME!" Without being able to see her yet, we know it's Charlotte, who sits in a recliner by the solarium's windows at the far end of the hall, footrest cranked up, hands gripping the armrests, eyes goggling in terror. Since she was admitted six months ago, Charlotte's cries have been a steady accompaniment to our visits with my mother.

Now ninety-five and fully engulfed within the wreckage of dementia, my mother has not seemed to notice the noise or the chaos it rained down around her. As never before in her life, she's calm. She doesn't lash out at Charlotte or try to drown her out with a blast from her own well-trained voice. There's usually a whimsical smile on my mother's face, the look of someone enchanted by an inner music and oblivious to distraction. As indeed she is. She registers almost nothing outside herself.

The last time we visited, her inner music was Jimmy Monaco's classic, "You Made Me Love You." Over and over as we sat with her, my mother gazed in my direction and sang about how I made her love me, though she didn't wanna do it. Her song selections during these visits often have an eerie resonance, as though chosen to deliver a last vital message to me. I know that can't be true, of course. Organic brain damage has left her incapable of such sophisticated cognition. She can't plan. She can't hold thoughts in mind or make the sort of conscious decisions that delivering such hurtful messages would involve. Her most commonly used phrase is *I don't know,* something she never would have admitted in her life. But given the richly marinated cruelty that once dominated her intimate behavior, this woman was not only capable of, but often did say things like *I never loved you. I never wanted you.* So when she sings "You Made Me Love You," I am engulfed by a sudden, irrational sadness.

It's nuts for me to continue holding on to this outdated version of my mother. I'm aware of that. It's also nuts for me to impute meaning or intent to her choice of songs. But this is still her familiar voice, this is still the familiar delivery of a lyric snippet laced with meaning, and I react physically, react immediately and without logic. Just as I hear the soft sigh of a door's tight seal as the sound of being consumed.

Today, as we reach the solarium where my mother should be sitting, we can't find her. We've already looked in her room, so we know she's not there either. When we turn to retrace our steps, an aide appears from inside a resident's room. She greets us with a smile. "Your mother is in the toilet."

Suddenly Charlotte cranks down her recliner's legs and hurtles toward us as though propelled by the chair's action, arms reaching out, fingers flexing. As the aide intercepts her, Charlotte shrieks "IN THE TOILET! REMEMBER THAT! YOUR MOTHER'S IN THE TOILET!"

The two of them move past us as though signaling the end of the show's opening act, at which point my mother emerges from a door behind them, led onstage by another aide. They shuffle together, holding hands like dancers performing the world's slowest fox trot. The aide drifts backward one measured step at a time, easing my mother into the solarium's autumn light. From behind us now, fading as she heads toward her room, Charlotte calls out "MOTHER! MOTHER IN THE TOILET! REMEMBER THAT!"

The aide arranges my mother at her customary table just west of the door and waves us over. My mother's head droops. We sit beside her and, as though she'd simply been waiting for her audience to settle down, my mother looks up and begins to hum. It's just a brief repetitive phrase that circles back to the beginning before I can recognize it. *Name that tune, Floyd!* I study her face, trying to see her in this moment, to be with her here rather than allow the past to intrude as it often does. Her expression is vague, as in a fading snapshot, and I'm shocked to see how much she resembles her father. And my brother in the months before his death. It's as though she has begun passing over to the other side, right before my eyes, a passage that has radically changed the way she looks. But then I realize it's because of the missing teeth. A few weeks ago, she lost her lower dentures, a common event on the Memory Impairment Unit. Since her diet consists exclusively of soft food, and the staff feels she's more comfortable without them and is likely to lose them again anyway, we've agreed for now not to replace the teeth.

"Hello, Mother. It's me." I pat her hands. She continues humming, nodding to the rhythm, and now I think I have the melody. She doesn't recognize me, and looks away. So I say, "Floyd. Your son."

There's still no response. Without thinking about it, and without giving them voice, I find myself filling in the lyrics of her song, "Shine On Harvest Moon."

"And I'm here too, Mother," Beverly says. "We're both here to visit you."

At that, my mother goes silent for a moment. She is mostly still, like a jukebox searching for its next record, then turns her head toward Beverly, smiles, and sings "Hey, good lookin', whatcha bah dee bah, something some something da dee dah for me?"

We sing along with her for a moment. At the same time, I hear Charlotte making her way back along the hall toward us, screaming "TOILET!" and I see a couple of my mother's fellow residents sidling up to our table to listen in on the concert. So I decide to introduce a topic for discussion, hoping to discourage the crowd by stopping the music.

"Tomorrow's Thanksgiving, Mother. Do you remember we used to have Thanksgiving at your brother's house in New York?"

She shakes her head. "I don't remember anything, so they say." Hearing her add "so they say" brings me to the edge of tears. She's so confused that she doesn't remember she can't remember, forgets her own forgetting, but somehow manages to remember that she's been told she forgets. Her tone is so soft and vulnerable, so unlike the way my mother would ever speak. If someone had the audacity to suggest that she didn't remember anything, she'd have turned on them viciously. *Don't you dare speak to me that way!* This simple openness, and this tone of benign acceptance, are new to my ears.

"Yes," I tell her, "we always used to visit Al for the holiday."

She shrugs, unconvinced, perhaps uninterested, so Beverly adds, "You loved him very much. You used to call him Albie."

"I don't think so," she says, though Beverly is right. "It was Algae."

"Albie," I say. "Albie and Marge."

"I'm always thinking of you, Margie!" my mother sings in reply.

Most of her recent songs, I realize, emerge from the same specific moment in time. Can this, I wonder, truly be what's happening in her shattered mind? She's somehow living again in the fall of 1931? Or are her song selections random, plucked from a deep and still-preserved remnant of memory that just happens to hold a cluster of tunes made popular in the same year, the same season? During a visit not long ago, my mother was singing a version of Herman Hupfeld's 1931 song, recorded that year by Rudy Vallee, "As Time Goes By." And "Margie" was a hit for Bix Beiderbecke in 1931, just before he died, and for Cab Calloway then as well. "You Made Me Love You" and "Shine On Harvest Moon" were both sung by Ruth Etting in *The Ziegfeld Follies of 1931*. This was the final *Ziegfeld Follies* show on Broadway, which ran for 164 performances between July and November, closing just before Thanksgiving. My mother told me many times that she used to see the *Follies* every year, intimating that Ziegfeld himself was grooming her to join the cast.

This period in late 1931 appears to be the moment my mother is locked into now, though it hardly seems possible for someone in her condition to be anywhere in time. In the fall of 1931 she was just turning twenty-one, just becoming an official adult. She lived with her parents in a New York City apartment, longing to be a singing star and to be courted by celebrities or distinguished men of wealth and aristocratic bearing. She was then, as she remained for the next seventy-five years, obsessed by two themes embodied in these songs and their performance: the difficulties of finding and sustaining the sort of romantic love for which she yearned, and the horror of being ignored, of not being bathed in the brightest light of public or private attention.

It was still possible for her to believe she might have a career on stage, singing lovesongs as Ruth Etting sang them. To believe, I suppose, that Potential loomed all around her despite the bank failures and food lines and grim prospects that defined the fall of 1931. Her stint as the Melody Girl of the Air was three years in the future.

It was also still possible for her to imagine for herself the sort of love in which a boy sighs, as in "Shine On Harvest Moon," because the girl he loves is by his side; the sort of love in which she would die for her sweetheart's brand of kisses, as in "You Made Me Love You." These were the hopes that fueled my mother's dreams as a young woman and her later fury as the housewife of a chicken butcher. She never let them go, hoarding and embellishing her youthful possibilities till they nestled like tinder in her emotional core.

For most of her life, my mother kept a box of photographs in the bottom of her lingerie drawer. Buried under the usual family snapshots, in a small and wrinkled manila envelope, were images of the suitors she rejected before marrying my father. After he died in 1961, she would often produce this collection as a kind of after-dinner entertainment, demanding that I look with her and listen to her lamentations. This one was now a famous attorney on the upper east side, upper west side, just off Central Park, and also in Boston and Hartford. He'd been a judge in the Bronx and a European diplomat, apparently at the same time. This one was an actor, a novelist, a concert violinist and pianist, a conductor and producer. This one was an inventor who spoke eleven languages fluently, and moved to both Greece and Spain the day after my mother turned down his proposal on the grounds that his parents had a terrible genetic disorder. Thereby saving my life. There was a Prince in exile, a dentist whose patients were limited to royalty—perhaps she met him through the Prince—and a man with such wealth that he didn't have to work, which is why she said No to his proposal, because who wanted a husband around the house all day. When I asked how she met my father and why she said Yes to him, she shook her head. *God knows.* Love, I came to understand from these photographs and the phantasmagoria that accompanied their display, was a matter of unrequited yearning. It had no present moment, no actual existence, no fulfillment. In fact, its very unattainability, except perhaps in the dreamworld of old standard songs, was what made love so miraculous. Such an obsession for her.

I know that I'm still trying to find meaning, or order, in her dwindling stock of songs, in her fragmentary remarks, the "memories" I always hope she will offer. I want something from her that she can't possibly give, that she never could have given, a coherent life story, maybe even a love-centered life story. One that included my father, if for only a brief moment when they were first together. One that included me. But the truth is, she never had much enthusiasm for or commitment to her lived life or its accurate recollection after the 1930s.

Now, when she finishes singing about Margie, she closes her eyes as though thinking, and asks me, "Is it classy?" Beverly and I look at each other. I'm not sure where this question came from, but despite what I know I'm still driven to treat it—like everything she says—as significant. My mother considered her brother and his wife, Albie and Marge, classy people. They were wealthy, had a Park Avenue apartment and also a home on a lake in upstate New York, attended cultural events. Perhaps my mother's statement was some sort of recollection triggered by our having mentioned them.

Into this brief, desperate silence comes a shout from the table behind us. "HELLO!" It's Bessie, whose room is across the hall from my mother's. She is turning the pages of a magazine and greeting each face she sees there.

My mother begins to sing again, moving deeper into "Shine On Harvest Moon," complaining now about not having had any loving since January, February, June, or July. She abandons the melody and speaks the lines, with dramatic emphasis, as though relating her recent experience: no loving since the beginning of the year.

Beverly and I, singing as a duet, try to lead my mother back to the song. After another round of the chorus my mother leans back and asks, "Do you agree with everything?"

I have no idea what this question means. Actually, I doubt it means anything. But looking around the solarium, listening to my mother and Charlotte and the other residents of the Memory Impairment Unit, recognizing all that is lost to time and illness, I know I must agree with everything. This is how it is.

Soon a cart laden with lunch trays begins to circulate through the room. Beverly and I, dazed by the repetition of lyrics, bizarre questions, and background cacophony, get up to leave. My mother doesn't notice, lost in her recapitulation of all the months that have gone by since she had any loving. As we exit the solarium, Charlotte returns to her recliner and screams "I FORGOT MY PURSE. HELP! I LOST MY FINGERS."

Exiting the nursing home's parking lot, I linger at the Stop sign, unable to remember which way I should turn. It's just a momentary confusion, hardly surprising in the aftermath of this visit, and Beverly doesn't even notice my hesitation. But as I make a left onto Boundary Avenue, I can feel my mother's presence in the car. *You should have turned right!*

It's as though I've contracted a touch of my mother's confusions. *In my do dah deuce coupe, la da de da do dah.* Then I remember her driving the great white Plymouth Fury she owned, a machine she blamed for always getting her lost.

I haven't thought about my mother and cars in years. She didn't learn to drive until she was forty-eight. That was in 1958, the year after we moved from Brooklyn to Long Beach, where there were no subways, the few buses stopped too many blocks from our house, and taxis had to be summoned by phone. Until then, living her entire life in various boroughs of New York City, she had no need to drive. No desire either: my mother aspired to being chauffeured. To sit in the back seat while a man in livery did her bidding. A chief complaint of her life with my father was that he refused to hire a car when they went to visit such well-do-to relatives as Al and Marge on Park Avenue. Instead, he raced through city streets behind the wheel of a black Buick, ash flying off his cigar whenever they hit a bump.

Once we'd settled in Long Beach, with both my father and brother commuting daily to Manhattan, my mother felt stranded. As a ten-year-old, I was of no use in transporting her. I can easily remember, forty-eight years later, the night she announced to the assembled family that she would learn to drive. It was a Friday because we were eating roast chicken and baked potato at the dining room table. When he heard what she said, my father stopped chewing and looked at each of us in turn, cheek bulging with meat. Then he finished chewing, crossed his fork and knife on the plate, and said "Who's going to teach you?"

Even I knew what he meant. He didn't wanna do it, didn't wanna do it.

My brother, now nineteen, said he'd teach her.

"You'll be sorry," my father said.

I don't remember how many evenings my brother took her out for lessons, but soon she was enrolled in driving school. She failed her first licensing test, but by late spring she'd passed. The first car she bought for herself, a few years later, was the Fury, a long vehicle whose grille looked like a frowning face. At just barely five feet tall, my mother seemed lost inside it. She had some trouble seeing beyond the edges when turning or parking and tended to scrape against parked cars, parking meters, lamp posts. The scratched surface would then canker and rust in the island's salt air. She also had some trouble with rules and procedures, unwilling to accept commands that she stop at the behest of silly red octagonal signs when it was obvious that no other cars were coming, to defer to arrows ordering her not to enter streets she wished to enter. She had no patience for traffic conditions intruding on her intentions.

As a driver, she routinely got lost. If a highway exit sign didn't specify the precise village she was looking for, she refused to take it. So unless her destination was a major town, she could travel for hours in the wrong direction before concluding that there was a problem. Driving from Long Beach north to nearby Baldwin, seeing only signs for Merrick or Freeport or New York, she would stay on the highway and cross from Long Island's south shore to its north shore before stopping to call home and complain.

"The stupid signs made me get lost."

"Where are you?"

"In a gas station."

"I mean in what town?"

She paused a moment, then said, "Shell."

Her wayward senses of direction, geography, and time didn't stop her from giving navigation advice when someone else was driving. *You should have turned right!* I always saw my mother's inability to find her way around as part of her disconnection from reality. The outside world never did matter much to her. Fantasy, fabricated memory, distortion: my mother seemed to live in another world entirely. It frustrated and often embarrassed me. I didn't see how lost she was in the world, as she is lost in it today, her mind swirling with confusions and retreating beyond dream, even beyond song.

As I drive west out of Portland, moving from Interstate 5 to 99W and on to state and county highways, traffic thins and each road is narrower the closer we get to home. My mother's directional commentary fades from mind, but not the image of her smiling vaguely, having no idea who I am, singing snatches of song from the 1930s. It's a long drive home, and whenever we return from these visits with my mother it feels as though I'm shedding the world as I move from city to town to village to the remote hillside where Beverly and I live in a small round house she built in the middle of twenty acres of oak, fir, maple, and wild cherry. It's a place my mother would have found deeply alien. The opposite of her aristocratic imaginings. But it has fulfilled my own longings, longings I didn't even know I had, for isolation and tranquility and quiet. *And I shall have some peace there, for peace comes dropping slow*, as Yeats said of his own longed-for spot. I see these trips back home as enacting my original escape west from my mother's place, from the noise and chaos of life in New York, life with her, to a space defined in part for me by its radical difference from all I grew up knowing.

Back home that afternoon, Beverly and I take a walk through the woods. This time of year, when the poison oak has died down, we like to follow deer trails that circle the landscape, clearing deadfall and dangling limbs as we go, making a viable path. Our kitten, Max, who is named after my mother's father, comes with us. He leaps from log to log, or races ahead of us through the brush, his youthful energy a tonic after we've spent time at the nursing home.

Softly singing my mother's songs, we exchange scraps of lyric till I get stuck in the chorus of "Shine On Harvest Moon." How does that line about snowtime end? It's no time to stay outdoors and croon? To stay outdoors after noon? Neither of us can remember. But we laugh at ourselves, having brought home a part of my mother, her way of conversing through song. When Beverly scratches a small rash on her arm, I sing "I've Got You Under My Skin"; when I tell her that Charlotte's screaming about my mother being in the toilet was unforgettable, she affirms, in her lovely alto, that it was unforgettable in every way. When singing of romance, my theme seems to be astonishment at finding love and a place for it in the world. Every time I think of my mother and her obsessive songs of failed romance, I think of how fortunate I am. As Beverly and I come back out of the woods, I break into one of my favorite love songs, scaring away a pair of dark-eyed juncos at the bird feeder, telling my wife that she is so beautiful to me.

The next time we visit my mother, we stop in to greet her nurse before entering the Memory Impairment Unit. Natalie has been caring for my mother since we brought her to the nursing home from New York in 2001. She smiles when I ask how things are going, and tells me that my mother hummed a little today as a guest pianist provided entertainment for the residents. But also that my mother is slowly, steadily fading away, sleeping more often during the afternoons, less and less able to summon up the will to move or to sing unless prompted.

"She's all right," Natalie says. "But she's leaving us."

This is something I've known for a while now. But as she has slowed down, lost weight, lost balance, she has done so in gradual, barely noticeable ways. She may be in the right lane, but she still hasn't found the exit she's after. I tell myself that, despite what Natalie says, despite how lost my mother is, the journey can still go on for quite a while.

There's a sign posted on the door to the Memory Impairment Unit warning visitors to check before opening it, in case a resident is waiting on the other side. People with Alzheimer's are sometimes compelled to wander, and a few of my mother's companions do tend to hover by the door. Beverly and I peer through the crack and see a familiar face peering back at us. In a moment, Charlotte has turned away and is walking back toward the solarium. "HELP ME! SOMEBODY HELP ME!"

We enter the unit, waiting till the door shuts behind us—in case Charlotte makes a dash for freedom—before moving down the hall. Again my mother is not in the solarium. The bathroom door is open, so we know she's not in there. She is, in fact, in her room, in her bed, asleep. She lies on her side, facing the wall, backed against a full-length body pillow. She is draped in orange and white alarm cords which will warn Natalie and the aides if my mother attempts to get out of bed, so they can rush to her and prevent her from falling.

Beverly and I look at each other, then back at my mother. We agree that we shouldn't wake her. Beverly gently covers my mother's exposed toes with the blanket that has slipped away. Before we leave, we lean over and kiss her. *Shine on!*

14

Travels in Lavender and Light

Beverly sat at her desk whispering to her laptop in French. *Le cheval saute.* On her screen, a horse jumped over a fence. I was on the couch reading Ernest Hemingway's *A Moveable Feast* so I, too, could be useful once we got to France. Hem found a good café on the Place St.-Michel and ordered rum St. James! I highlighted it with yellow marker. As a cat jumped off a chair, Beverly whispered *Le chat saute.*

For almost a year, we prepared for this trip in our customary fashion. She examined maps and guidebooks and Web sites to plan our routes and destinations. "I think we should see the Abbaye de Sènanque, near Gordes, don't you?" she said. "It's famous for its lavender fields."

"Absolutely," I said. "And when we're in Paris, let's be sure to go to a couple of English-language bookstores."

She researched bed and breakfast options, inspecting room layouts, furnishings, and views. She arranged our flights and rental car, figured out the sights to see and the sequence in which to see them, factoring in time of day and the consequent variations in light or crowds. She thought about the need to rest and avoid sensory overload. Beckoning me over to the dining room table, where a Michelin map was spread beneath the dangling light, she traced the countryside with her finger and said, "We should probably spend the first night somewhere here in Burgundy, so we don't have to drive all the way to Provence after the long flight."

"For sure. And let's go to a couple of English-language bookstores when we get to Paris."

She considered weather forecasts and analyzed our clothing needs. She studied at her computer and soon could read French menus, travel instructions for the Parisian subway system, whole blocks of French text about châteaux near Blois. She said things to me in French that sounded intimate, even titillating, but meant that the window was open or the restaurant didn't accept credit cards. Meanwhile, I reread Hemingway. I read Zola and Camus and Houellebecq. I bought but didn't read *Swann's Way*. All set.

Neither of us had wanted to travel to Europe again this year. We'd been to Italy for a month last year and were eager to spend our summer at home. As I near sixty, I find myself exhausted by travel and approach the prospect of a trip like the speaker of Elizabeth Bishop's poem, "Questions of Travel," who arrives at her destination saying, "Think of the long trip home. / Should we have stayed at home and thought of here?"

But it had taken us only moments to say Yes when I'd been invited to teach at the Paris Writers Workshop. After all, I'd never been to France, and this was such an unexpected opportunity, a kind of gift it felt wrong to refuse. Beverly, who had been to France twenty years earlier, longed to return. In the time since that visit, she'd become an Impressionist landscape painter. So she was eager to see and photograph the Provençal lavender fields in all kinds of light. They should be blooming when we're there. Also sunflower fields and poppy fields, Mont Ventoux, the grand summer landscape of Cézanne and Van Gogh, of Signac, Derain, Braque, Dufy. We decided to spend some time driving around France and hanging out in Paris before the workshop began. We allocated five days for Provence. She wanted to see the Loire Valley and visit Monet's garden at Giverny. Three days. Then on to Paris, where I would work with a dozen English-speaking students in a room smelling of coffee and croissants, located above a corner cafè.

Sounded good. Time in the countryside, time in Paris: a perfect balance. And full of secret pleasures. For instance, I love to drive backroads with Beverly beside me hunting for scenes to photograph. She puts me through all sorts of challenging maneuvers when she spots a promising photo-op: sudden stops, instant turns, daring reverses. Concentrating, she radiates excitement, and I always prefer to look at her rather than the scene she's shooting. There's plenty of time to study the scenery when her photos get developed.

Our brief road trip would be a great way to arrive in the City of Lights refreshed, all Frenched-up and ready to teach. It even had an Impressionist bonus once we settled in Paris: the studio apartment we'd been offered on the Rue Bonaparte was located in the building where Manet was born. My favorite painter, a man whose final burst of passionate still-life painting overcame the crippling of his body and gave me hope when my own body was changed by illness. And then there were the English-language bookstores to visit, with books from the British and Irish publishers I can't find at home.

But I probably shouldn't have read so much Camus. In his *Notebooks 1935–1942*, he writes that what gives value to travel is fear, the feeling of being so far from the safety of home and old habits. "At that moment we are feverish but also porous, so that the slightest touch makes us quiver to the depths of our being. We come across a cascade of light, and there is eternity." I must admit that despite the business about cascading light, this didn't sound appealing to me. I didn't want to travel in order to feel fear, quiver at the slightest touch, and be any more porous than I already am.

As the trip neared, I had alarming dreams. In one, an aproned

French chef, armed with his cleaver and wearing a soldier's helmet instead of a chef's hat, screamed at me for being an American, repeating as he chopped apart the table, *How could you re-elect this man Bush?* In another, clearly influenced by Camus, I was standing on a bridge over the Seine as river water rushed through the sieve my body had become.

A few days before we departed, with luggage spread across the floor, language practice complete, student manuscripts read and commented on, Beverly and I sat together on the couch watching the sun set.

"I'll miss this," one of us said. As usual, I was in my Questions of Travel mode, experiencing anticipatory homesickness and porosity aversion.

But, I thought, rallying, there'll be gorgeous sunsets in Provence. It'll be a good change of pace. I added a cool breeze on the Loire with a bottle of local rosé and a platter of cheeses, added night life in Paris. *Voilà.*

We nodded together. Then we said, in unison, what we always say when we leave here. "It'll be good to be home."

If it weren't broken, the Airbus on which we were scheduled to fly to Paris would seat all 335 passengers now scattered around the departure gate at the Detroit airport. So would the spare Airbus we kept hearing about, parked in a distant hangar and also needing repair. Northwest Airlines's mechanics were trying to fix both planes simultaneously. We got updates on our flight's status every twenty minutes, which told us they'd know more about our flight's status in twenty minutes. The subtext was eerie: we'd be using whichever defective craft first got declared airworthy by an airline that badly wanted to avoid putting 335 passengers up in a Detroit motel overnight.

Cheaper to keep us here through the night, heads resting on carry-on luggage, folded jackets, companions' laps, receiving periodic encouragement. Northwest personnel began handing out blankets and a few pillows. They distributed free international phone cards good for five minutes of panicky bilingual chatter about delayed arrivals. They produced a wheeled cart bearing free airline snacks, and announced that because supplies were short, women and children should eat first. For a few minutes the space around us filled with sounds of savagely torn paper wrappers and the crunching of peanuts or pretzels. There was juice. Among adults, there was general discussion of the need for hard liquor.

As the fifth hour began, we were told that we'd depart from a different gate if the spare plane was fixed first. But we should remain where we were for now. Further updates in twenty minutes. Beverly turned on her side and made a serious effort at sleep. On the floor beside her, I stared at the ceiling, unable to block out the repeated three-note giggle of a teenage girl telling her traveling companions about her boyfriend's family. The giggles erupted every ten to twelve seconds.

I might have been even more worried about our plane if I weren't so tired. It was almost 2:00 a.m. Wednesday and way past our bedtime, even back on Pacific time. Northwest WorldGateway had closed down. Except for the 335 of us at the gate, and a few terminal employees, the place was empty. All bathrooms had been sealed by tape and looked like crime scenes as workers cleaned them. A vacant two-hundred-passenger tram ran back and forth along the concourse ceiling every two and a half minutes.

Our Jet Lag Prevention Plan had been so clever. For the last few days, after our ritual viewing of the sunset from our living room, we'd been going to sleep earlier and earlier, resetting internal clocks to approximate French time. We'd woken up at 3:00 a.m. on travel day, fresh from eight hours of sleep, bought food at the Portland airport, and ate a mid-afternoon dinner on board the flight to Detroit. When we heard about a twenty-minute delay here, we decided to risk taking our various herbal sleeping potions at the departure gate, preparing ourselves to sleep all the way to Paris. Now, as another 3:00 a.m. approached, our internal clocks had gone haywire.

So had the mellowness that all our planning was meant to achieve. We'd done everything we could to ease the chaos associated with travel, but there's no way to plan for broken airbuses. Still, a delayed connecting flight was hardly a vacation-killer. Happens to everyone. And this situation in Detroit was better than the one we experienced in Cincinnati seven years ago, when we arrived at the departure gate to find the plane for our Pittsburgh connecting flight surrounded by pieces of its own engines.

The spare plane won the repair derby. We took off six hours late.

By the time we picked up our rental car at Charles de Gaulle airport, we had only four hours to reach our first night's Burgundian destination, Beaune, before the hotel's gates closed for the night. It was, according to our route planner, about 210 miles from Paris, an estimated three-hour-and-twenty-minute drive. If traffic wasn't too bad, we thought we still might make it. But we couldn't figure out how to exit the airport.

At first, we couldn't even figure out how to exit the rental car parking lot. Signs directed us to a traffic circle where additional signs, large and colorful, were resolutely silent about how to get where we need to go. The problem wasn't linguistic. Beverly could read what information there was. Hell, I could too. But the information was wildly incomplete, didn't correlate to the map she was holding or the written instructions she had downloaded, and the traffic was heavy, and we'd been traveling for nearly thirty-two hours, and the late afternoon temperature was ninety-two degrees, and so we drove the little Renault Modus around the traffic circle twice trying to make sense of things. Then, knowing which roads we didn't want, we chose the option that seemed least wrong. Which turned us straight north on a small road toward Epiais-Les-Louvres when we knew we needed to go straight south on a huge motorway toward Dijon and Beaune.

We got back to the airport and made another circle, then found the road we wanted at the same time as the rest of Paris rush-hour traffic. This left us little to do but laugh as we drifted toward Burgundy, watching only time race by.

Neither of us needed to mention that the trip so far had been consistent with my checkered record as a traveler. In 1988, I contracted the virus that targeted my brain on a flight from Oregon to Washington DC. My doctors believe it was carried on the plane's recirculating air system. During the ongoing process of recovery, I've tried not to view travel as jinxed by that one flight. But a few years ago, at age fifty-five and after teaching for the Mid-Atlantic Creative Nonfiction Writing conference in Towson, Maryland, I contracted chicken pox, most likely on the flight home, that bloomed ten days later. Then there were the lesser foul-ups, what I thought of as the Floyd Factor, which tended to override Beverly's wise and careful preparation. On our honeymoon, for instance, boarding a local train in Genoa, I got my vast backpack stuck between the doors as they closed and the train moved toward a tunnel. Half in, half out, cane pointing heavenward, I was unable to free myself. Beverly tugged at the doors, then yanked at a lever beside them, then attracted the attention of a group of teens who helped her pry the doors apart just before we reached the tunnel, and a conductor arrived to scream at us through the next two stations because we yanked the lever. In Germany, depending as we were on my limited language skills, we nearly ended up at a poultry yard (*geflügelhof*) instead of an airport (*flughafen*). In Ireland, I recommended a shortcut across bogland and sank to kneecap and cane-top before taking a dozen steps. In New York, where I grew up and knew my way around, I led us from Union Square north to the Empire State Building before realizing we weren't actually headed south toward Greenwich Village. North and south did seem to be issues for me. Little wonder I preferred to stay home. I often felt too neurologically compromised to travel well, and one of my deepest concerns was that I would get lost, would lose myself, in the strangeness of foreign travel.

By 10:30, we reached the outskirts of Beaune. Using interior lights to study directions provided by the hotel, we zoomed through town and out the other side without finding the place. Beverly made the first call on our new international cell phone, reached the hotel proprietor, explained to her where we were—in front of a different hotel—and kept talking to her as we followed directions back into the town's center, then under a railroad overpass, and to the front gate a scant fifteen minutes before closing time.

We were shown to our room. The proprietor pointed a remote control device at the air-conditioner mounted high on the wall, where a television would be if this were a hospital room, and turned the delicate machine on. It was quiet, but that may have been because it barely worked. When the proprietor left, Beverly and I looked at each other and yawned. *We're in France!*

"Did she just say we only get eight minutes worth of cold air?" I asked.

"Not quite. She said breakfast at eight."

I think it was on the first evening in Provence that I was bitten on the side of my leg by a spider. I didn't notice the bite till the next evening because water trapped in my ear was occupying so much attention. I got water trapped in my ear because we went swimming in the pool at L'ermitage, our bed and breakfast near Vaison-la-Romaine, where the temperature on the evening we arrived was ninety-four degrees.

Normally, I would sit at a pool's edge with my feet in the water and watch Beverly swim. A former competitive racer who once held

the Oregon state record for ten-year-old girls in the fifty-yard butterfly, she is so graceful and powerful in the water that it's even more
compelling for me than watching her take photographs. But I was
desperate in the Provençal heat, and our room had no air conditioning, and the pool was situated to catch direct sunlight till almost
bedtime, so full-body-immersion swimming seemed irresistible.

I hadn't realized there was so much wax built up in my ear. I
spent hours digging around in the canal with a finger, then with a
Q-tip, trying to liberate the water and creating a miserable impression of the way Americans behave when they greet new people or
eat French food.

It had been a good day. Our Modus was air conditioned, and the
long drive down to Provence was a masterpiece of navigation. I realized that our best pre-trip purchases were three vast Michelin
maps. With Provence and Côte d'Azur spread across her lap like an
antimacassar, Beverly guided us off the Autoroute du Soleil near
Malataverne and to our first lavender fields, in Côtes du Rhone
country along the small road from Clansayes to Richerenches. We
could not believe our luck. In full bloom, the fields offered an ex-
travaganza of form and color, their range of purples softening or
thickening according to the angle of light, some arrayed in orderly
rows and others in sensuous curves, some set off by stone buildings and others alone in their glory.

Despite the heat, things were going splendidly as we settled into
our room and spent some time in the pool. L'ermitage, owned by
friends of friends back in Oregon, was a two-hundred-year-old farmhouse on the slopes of a medieval hilltop village, Crestet. It had apri-
cot and cherry orchards, a small vineyard, a view of Mont Ventoux,
English-speaking owners, and we were in a green room with a view
of the courtyard. After our swim, we showered and walked down
the hill to a restaurant for dinner.

Then, however, we ate, and the evening began to turn strange.

Beverly's appetizer, a triangular onion tart shaped like a pizza slice, was the best item we ordered. My mixed buffet appetizer, tasting and looking like a collection of chef's discards, came from a table filled with fly-specked plates in a cubicle located near the bathroom. We set aside Beverly's main dish after one taste each, squid that resembled something out of a Jules Verne novel rather than the crisp tidbits of calamari we were anticipating, and we ate only the sauce accompanying my multi-cooked pork.

After dinner, we drove into Vaison-la-Romaine searching for an internet cafè and, along a narrow back street, came face to face with a parade of girls on horseback. I reversed into an alley and we got out to watch. The girls, some as young as three or four, rode past, dressed in elaborate Renaissance costumes and trailed by rows of men playing pipes, then rows of men firing guns into the air, and finally four monks. The last monk turned to look at us and winked. The moment felt simultaneously celebratory and sinister.

All the next day, the temperature hovered around one hundred degrees. From late morning till early evening we remained in the tiny front seat of our air conditioned car, driving, stepping outside for brief moments to take photographs or buy a six-pack of bottled water and a lunch we ate in the car. Only a few of the lavender fields east of Crestet were in bloom, though we went as far as Banon and came back through Sault, where the owner of L'ermitage was sure we'd find them in full glory.

While drying myself off after a second evening shower I noticed the red blotch on my leg. At first I thought the mark on my leg was heat rash. Either that or some previously unknown, instantaneous form of melanoma. But it was round and neat, several shades of vermilion, and it expanded every hour or so as I kept watch. In the one calm mini-micrometer of my mind I knew it was an insect bite, probably from a spider because of its shape. I stood there working a finger into my ear and vaguely remembering a stinging sensation the evening before, when we were sitting under a tree after swimming. Couldn't be a deadly spider, since I was still alive twenty-four hours later. *Get a grip, Floyd!* Only a few days into the trip, and I was already the fearful, quivering, porous mess Camus had written about. "Travel," as he also said in his notebooks, "brings us back to ourselves." I hoped this day's sorry self wasn't my trip's ultimate destination.

It was becoming clear to me that the farther I traveled into the French countryside, the deeper I was going into my own head and its landscape of illness obsession, of anxiety about injury and malign chance. Look, even the French spiders hate Americans!

Saturday was market day in nearby Ste. Cecile-les-Vignes, and we started our morning there at a pharmacy. They should have what I need for my leg and ear. Since neither of us knew quite how to phrase my problems, I turned sideways and pointed to the bite, then yanked on my left earlobe and stuck a finger in the canal. The woman at the counter looked shocked for me, or at me, then nodded and handed over a tube of antibiotic cream and a bottle of ear wax softener.

We drove on to Sèguret and Gigondas, and in deepening heat turned north, where we'd had the best luck finding lavender fields in bloom. We came to several fields with row after row of brilliant sunflowers, their heads quite sensibly and uniformly turned away from the blazing sun. Their yellows combined miles later with vivid lavender and the occasional red poppy to form a surreal palette. They were, I thought, this week's true colors. Climbing a narrow road on Montagne d'Autuche, where I honked my way around each curve, we were overtaken by a balding cyclist. Just watching him made me crank up the air conditioner.

Sunday in Carpentras, an elderly woman smelling faintly of lavender, and with a smile like a cascade of light, helped bring me back to myself again. The self who lived open to the world. She did this with an unexpected act of kindness that penetrated the shield of my travel anxieties.

She was strolling home with her neighbor, two white-haired women in church-going suits despite the heat, when Beverly approached to ask for help. We'd come to Carpentras to find another pharmacy, because the antibiotic cream we'd bought in Ste. Cecile-les-Vignes had done nothing for me and we finally realized I needed an antihistamine instead. Carpentras, a town of thirty thousand people, was certain to have numerous pharmacies. Why, it was famous for the eighteenth-century cupboards in its Hôtel Dieu that housed a well-preserved pharmacopeia from those old days. Drug Pride. It seemed a good omen.

As soon as we'd passed through the central town square with its great stone fountain, we saw the familiar green-and-white cross pharmacy sign and pulled into an empty parking lot. The place was closed on Sunday, as are most pharmacies in France. But one is always open in each town and the trick is finding the right one. That's when Beverly approached the two women.

After halting discussion, one led Beverly back through the parking lot to the shop's closed door, and pointed to a small sign listing that day's open pharmacy. Then she explained in rapid French how to get there. Seeing that the complicated directions might be too much for us, she waved good-bye to her friend, walked over to our car, opened the back door, and got in. She said to Beverly that she would guide us, as long as we brought her back to this same spot afterward.

I kept turning around to smile and needlessly translate for Beverly her simple instructions, which were made clear to me only because she pointed as she spoke. *À droite.* "To the right." *Tout droit,* which seemed to mean "straight ahead" though I translated it as "make two rights" and nearly caused a crash. I couldn't get enough of seeing the woman's round, open face, the returning smile, the sense of wonder that flowed through me when I tried to imagine myself doing what she was doing. *À gauche*, she said, pointing to the pharmacy on the left side of a street we'd never have found by ourselves. Then she came inside with us. Maybe it was her silent presence, a symbol of good fortune made visible even to me, that caused the pharmacist to understand Beverly's description and my sign language. We got the right remedy this time. As we drove our guide back to the place where she'd joined us, I rubbed cream on the spider bite. It was absorbed quickly.

By morning the spider bite began to recede. Since my ears were no longer plugged, I was running out of maladies to worry about. But there was still the heat. Next morning we headed north toward the Loire Valley, a seven-hour drive, and seemed to drag the torrid sun of Provence along with us. It was still ninety degrees at 8:00 p.m. when we ate dinner alfresco in Meung, the town where Alexandre Dumas' *The Three Musketeers* opens and young D'Artagnan is first seen. Nothing stirred. The wine, a local rosé like the one I'd imagined as we prepared to leave home, seemed actually on the brink of boiling.

We decided to rest the next day, sitting under trees by the Loire and chatting with other guests at the bed and breakfast, watching the two resident dogs, young Vasco and aging Lilly, as they kept shifting positions to avoid the sun. Late that afternoon, the heat broke.

We got up early the next morning and drove three hours north to Giverny, arriving at the nearly vacant parking lot across from Monet's home at 10:00, just as the place opened. We toured the garden and house, and Beverly took three rolls of film before we left to walk the streets of town and eat lunch outdoors at the Musée d'Art Américain. On the long way back to Meung we stopped to photograph poppy fields, and I even got out of the car to join Beverly at the roadside.

We were happy to surrender our rental car and begin living the city life in Paris. Despite its diet heavy with butter and cheeses and eggs and fat-wrapped patés and sauces, we understood why so many Parisians seemed lean. It was liberating to walk everywhere. Through the weekend, we visited the museums, walked through the gardens, found the bookstores. Each time we wanted to return to our studio apartment, we had to climb seven flights of circular stairs, each flight narrowing until the final turn, just wide enough for our shoulders to pass.

The studio itself was long and narrow, created from three maids' rooms in the attic above the owner's main apartment, and in places the ceiling was so slanted that even I knocked my head on it. This was a novel experience for me.

The night before my first Paris Writers Workshop class, Beverly and I strolled from our apartment through St. Germain des Pres to the Jardin du Luxembourg and up toward Montparnasse. Unintentionally, we'd ended up in the neighborhood where I'd be teaching.

Beverly knew that I was worried about getting lost while walking or riding the bus to class. She suggested that we walk back directly to our apartment so I could visualize my way and even take notes if I wished. We went down the Rue de Sèvres to the Rue du Four to the Rue de Rennes. I noted the landmarks at corners where I needed to turn, a park here, a Gap store there. We crossed Boulevard St. Germain and passed right by Hemingway's beloved café, Les Deux Magots, which I'd read about and highlighted in yellow so long ago, then entered the Rue Bonaparte. What next, a jumping horse or cat?

In the morning, I got lost walking to work. Maybe it was the distraction of the rain. Rain! Despite the map in my briefcase and the handwritten notes in my pocket, I missed two turns and finally realized that I was headed the wrong way when I crossed the Rue de Vaugirard, a name I recognized from our previous night's wandering through the Jardin du Luxembourg.

But it really didn't matter. I stood under an awning to study the map, figured out how to get to the workshop office, and made it there in time for my class to begin. Afterward, I walked back to our apartment and along the way bought a ham sandwich on baguette. Eating it on the go, like so many Parisians I'd seen since arriving, I realized that I was singing between bites. I climbed the stairs and was let in to the room by Beverly, who had remained indoors in the rain, painting a few scenes from our travels.

On our last night in Paris, with luggage spread across the apartment floor, the workshop complete, Beverly's paintings carefully wrapped, we sat together on the fold-out bed watching the sun set. The view was of church steeples and rooftops, scudding clouds, one thick-leaved tree. We could hear buses accelerate from the stop near our building, motor scooters dashing between cars that honked as the light changed.

"Will you miss this?" one of us said.

We might not miss it, we agreed, but we'd remember it. We nodded together. Then we said, in unison, "It'll be good to be home."

But getting out of Paris proved to be harder and even more frustrating than arriving. The itinerary supplied by our travel agent told us our flight would depart from Terminal One at Charles de Gaulle airport, so that's where we asked our cab driver to leave us. Though there were no roadway signs listing which airlines were located in which terminals, I never thought to doubt we were going to the right place.

Beverly and I stood flanking our five pieces of luggage, staring at the departure board. Nothing said Detroit. Nothing said Northwest Airlines. Had we been seeking Air Gabon, Pakistan International Airlines, Gulf Air, or Qatar Airlines, we were in the right place. We could fly Yemenia or Kuwait Airways or take Pulkovo Aviation to St. Petersburg. After ten minutes of searching, we found an information booth where our mix of French, English, and sign language produced the advice that we should take a shuttle bus to Terminal Two, a fifteen-minute ride away.

On the bus, we came to understand that there are, in fact, a half dozen Terminal Twos. Hall A to Hall E. In other airports, these six "Halls" would be called what they are, terminals. Beverly asked the driver which Terminal Two housed Northwest and was answered with a shrug. He said, she thought, that we should try the first stop.

Terminal Two A would have been the right one if we were flying Air Madagascar or Cathay Pacific. We could have gone to Mumbai on Air France or Air India. But no, not Detroit, not Northwest. Beverly managed to find someone who understood where we were going and told us to go to Terminal Two E. He said we could walk there in about ten minutes, but with our luggage maybe we should take the shuttle bus. We did, and it was a good thing because walking there along a freeway would have taken a good half hour.

Terminal Two E is the one whose roof collapsed in May 2004. It was newly reopened now, with two vast lines of passengers snaking around each other toward the single security gate. We made it through to our plane shortly before boarding time, and precisely twenty-four hours after leaving our apartment in Paris we arrived at our house in the woods.

It was almost midnight. A clear, starry sky was visible through our skylight, and a tree frog croaked at the moon. We moved around the house with our heads cocked at an angle, still trained by the slanted ceilings of the Rue Bonaparte apartment, and did not have to say it was good to be home. Instead, one of us pointed toward the moonlit forest and said, *Voilà!* and the other said, "Let's unpack in the morning."

15

Jambon Dreams

I t was a winter night in 1952. My brother was thirteen and fam-
ished, though we'd finished dinner only an hour earlier. He tiptoed into the kitchen and approached a pan of leftover stuffed cabbage cooling on the counter. I followed, wearing black Hopalong
Cassidy pajamas and an empty holster on my hip, toy six-gun cocked
in my hand. I was five and learning how to be a food thief.

It was vital to know the whereabouts of the authorities: my mother sat at her desk in the foyer, talking on the phone, and my father
slept.

"Don't make a sound," Philip whispered.

The kitchen window was steamed over, but I could still see lights
from apartments that faced ours in the east Flatbush neighborhood.
I could hear traffic below on Lenox Road. The room smelled of tomato, ground beef, onion, and the rank biology of cabbage wrap-
pings cooked so long that the outer leaves flopped into the sauce. My
parents called this concoction *galooptchy*, and loved to eat it for days
as leftovers. Those loosed leaves were Philip's target. If he could be
delicate enough in his touch so that nothing looked out of place afterward, and careful not to drip sauce once he'd liberated the goods,
he could pilfer a few and eat them without getting caught.

He didn't particularly like cabbage leaves. But he liked foiling our parents' plans, he liked taking forbidden food, and he needed the practice. I was there to appreciate the moves.

The week before, I'd witnessed his failed Velveeta Caper. My mother had brought home the smallest available block of the cheese, Philip's favorite, and placed it on the refrigerator shelf with a warning: *this has to last the whole week.* When she'd gone downstairs to visit her friend Ann, Philip opened the box, unfolded the foil packaging, and cut chunk after chunk, devouring each one plain, without crackers or bread, without offering any to me, and without pause, until just one thin slice was left. Then he crumpled up wax paper and shaped the mass into a rectangle, stuffed it against the remaining slice, re-folded the packaging, and slipped the box top back into place.

"Don't touch that," he said. "I'll finish the last piece in a week."

Of course, it had been a trap. Food provision, like food thievery, was a highly nuanced business in our family. As soon as she came home, my mother checked the refrigerator. She touched the Velveeta box, which yielded to her finger's pressure, and screamed. She demanded our presence before her. *I hope you two enjoyed your feast!* Philip ate no dinner that night. Neither did I, his ravenous sidekick.

But he got away—we both got away—with his cabbage operation. I remember that near the end of it, rapt in his work, Philip did drip a freckle of sauce onto the linoleum. Like our mother, I raced to grab a paper towel, gasping instead of screaming. After I'd cleaned the floor, he winked at me. Then we tiptoed back to our room.

One Sunday morning in 1956, my father woke me and Philip by slapping our feet with a spatula. He wore his chef's apron, and stood between our beds with his right index finger pressed to his lips. *Shhhhh. Don't wake her.*

I'd never seen my father cook, and didn't know he could. He sold the stuff that other people cooked, he ate stuff that other people cooked, and I figured he had nothing to do with what happened in between. The apron, I thought, was only for when he served drinks before a dinner party.

Usually, we had Sunday breakfast at Toomey's Diner, but this morning it was raining, and he'd heard that Toomey's was closed all week because of a death in the family, and since we'd all be driving up to Connecticut later that morning to visit my mother's cousins, we couldn't do our usual Sunday outing.

"Breakfast in ten minutes," he whispered. "Get yourselves ready."

Soon there was an alarming smell from the kitchen. I looked at Philip and he smiled, raised his eyebrows, and rubbed his hands together. "Baloney and eggs!"

This was another revelation for me. I hadn't known it was possible to cook baloney, or to eat baloney with eggs, and survive. Besides, such a combination might be against the rules.

We weren't exactly kosher in the house, though our father's was a kosher market, its poultry slaughtered according to the rules. We routinely mixed meat and dairy at the same meal, and didn't keep separate meat and dairy dishes, or buy specially blessed foods, so I figured kosher only applied when people visited other people's homes. I knew it didn't apply to meals eaten in restaurants, unless we were in a restaurant with family or friends who kept their homes kosher. I knew about the restaurant exception to kosher rules because we could have pork in restaurants. The truth is, I lived for ham: ham steak, country ham, Virginia ham, fried ham, sliced ham, ham with eggs, ham in baked beans. We could sometimes have pork at home, but only when our father brought fresh pork sausage from the Italian butcher next door to his market. Probably keeping kosher, when it came to pork in the home, only applied when people got their food from strangers. At home, we ate only beef hot dogs or cold cuts, except when at Ebbets Field or when the grocery store had a special on bratwurst or braunschweiger, so the rules about pork also had something to do with sports and economics. Similarly, we ate shrimp and lobster in Chinese restaurants, but not at home, so I figured that the Chinese had special access to kosher shellfish. To poultry as well, since their restaurants were my father's best wholesale customers, in which case it was all right to ignore the fact that their kitchens were contaminated, or *trayf,* as my parents called anything non-kosher when we weren't eating it. Clams we ate only at restaurants located near the ocean, which led me to believe that clams were kosher if consumed within sight of their homes. The rules were sometimes a little hard to follow.

But my shock over baloney and eggs wasn't primarily about violations of rules. It was about the strangeness of eating baloney and eggs together, even if the combination was technically permissible. The smell, and the way the meat curled away from the eggs no matter how I tried to flatten it, certainly suggested they didn't belong on the same plate.

I was learning that most of my assumptions about food were false. Every time I thought I understood what we did and didn't do, something strange would occur. There seemed to be few guiding principles other than stealth and the violation of all rules. Eat what you want, especially what you're not supposed to, whenever the opportunity presents itself.

When my father sold his poultry market in 1957, we celebrated with a series of dinners. One for his employees and best customers at a restaurant in Red Hook. Another for his fellow butchers, bakers, and produce men on Union Street, where almost every guest had provided one of the menu's fresh items, from the mussels posillipo and garlic bread to the roasted meats and desserts. There was a dinner for the Skloot uncles and aunts and cousins, held at our grandmother's home because she was the one who had gotten the family started in the poultry business originally. We also had dinner at the home of the Italian family who bought the market. And dinner for just the four of us, a final feast shortly before we moved away from Brooklyn, featuring poultry my father had killed and cleaned with his own hands. My mother, who had been urging him to sell his market for the last three years, burst into tears when she set the heaped platter down. She left the room for a minute or two, then as we were about to begin eating that last dinner, my father took off his glasses and wept. It was the only time I ever saw him cry, and it made me cry. My brother laughed, but then his laughter converted to crying too. We sat there, all four in tears, watching the pullet give off steam and sag into its bed of roasted fennel.

Like so many families, we celebrated holidays, events, and achievements by eating. For us, though, as with the rules of keeping kosher, these celebrations had fine calibrations governed by complex regulations. If I brought home an especially good report card from school, we would go out to eat, but not at an Italian or seafood restaurant, the most expensive cuisines we liked. Grades might be worth dinner at a diner, or a sit-down deli feast, but not fancy chicken cacciatore or fresh lobster. After the first week of my brother's new job at a clothing factory, we ate at a restaurant in the west end of town famous for its spare ribs, but we weren't allowed to order appetizers and skipped dessert. The end of a week of continual rain was worth a Chinese dinner, but only combination plates, not separate main dishes, which were proper for adult birthdays and certain holidays. When my mother got a singing role in a community theater production, we had steaks all around. Some visitors merited better meals than others when we went out together. My Uncle Al and Aunt Margie got the full Italian restaurant treatment. My father's eldest sister, a distinguished interior decorator, and her well-to-do husband, got to eat at Meyer & Kronke, which my mother called a four-star Manhattan restaurant stranded in Oceanside. But my father's middle sister and her traveling salesman husband, on the rare occasions we ate with them, got the small café with its burgers and sandwiches.

If we celebrated by eating, and entertained by eating, we also grieved by eating. The day my father died, only Philip and I were home when the phone call came, and our first act was to open the refrigerator and slap together roast beef sandwiches. A day later, family and friends returned home with us from the cemetery and shared a catered feast. Kosher, from the restaurant on Park Street, because my father's mother and eldest brother would be with us. Wearing a black dress and demure white apron, Hannah, the woman hired by my mother to cook and clean, took me into a corner and whispered, "You Skloots is the eatin'est people I ever saw." Then she continued rushing through the living room, dodging mourners, carrying heavy trays.

She was right, and I've remembered her observation for forty-six years. We ate a lot, we ate meaningfully, and we ate recklessly. A family given to heart disease, strokes, and diabetes, we gorged on fatty foods, salty foods, sweets. We often ate with abandon, especially Philip and I, down at our corner of the table, grabbing for dishes if they weren't passed quickly enough, snaring morsels from one another's plates, licking our fingers to lift a few final crumbs of bread.

Meals could be a time of peace, if the food satisfied in quality and amount, if everyone's mood was stable, if the stars were aligned. But meals could also be a battleground, every member of the family looking out for himself only, seizing what they wanted, hunching over the plate to guard their food. Tempers could flare, the day's misdemeanors and insults and losses tossed into the mix as forks shoved food into mouths between accusations and recriminations.

Food mattered to us, to me, in ways that evolution may not have intended. It sure seemed to be the center of all attention.

"Don't get any on the seat," Philip said.

I leaned farther outside the car and said, "Don't worry, I know what I'm doing."

"And don't get any on the door, either."

As usual, Philip and I were trading *don'ts* as we ate. We were hunkered back-to-back in his new, white 1961 Plymouth Valiant, eating ham sandwiches on loaves of crusty bread. The car's front doors were wide open wide, oil and vinegar dressing dripped down our chins to land between our feet on the asphalt, and bread crumbs exploded all around us. We didn't look around when we talked, and we didn't stop chewing, but none of that mattered because we didn't have to hear each other to conduct this conversation.

"Don't talk when you eat," I said. "You spray food all over the place."

"Don't be a wise guy. Last week, there was mustard all over the floor on your side."

I leaned farther out the door, held the sandwich at arm's length, stretched my neck like a goose in flight, and took another bite. "Don't distract me."

That sunny Saturday afternoon still lingers in memory because it was the one time my brother broke with his routine. Instead of the usual hero sandwich, he'd ordered what I'd ordered, ham and Swiss with extra lettuce and dressing.

"Don't kid yourself," he said as we neared the end of our meals. "This isn't a real sandwich, it's an hors d'oeuvre."

Lacking the proper variety of meats, containing only one kind of cheese, missing the pickles and tomatoes and onions and peppers, my regular Saturday lunch seemed like diet food to Philip. A semi-sandwich. But it was the kind I loved, the kind I'd even begun to dream about.

Halfway through lunch, he began the ritual quiz: "Okay, what's a hero sandwich called in Philadelphia?"

"A hoagie."

"In Boston?"

"Grinder."

"What about Chicago?"

"A sub."

"And why do they call it a sub?"

"Because it's shaped like a submarine."

He nodded. Sea gulls circled above us, coming in off the bay just beyond the playground where we were parked. If one landed near us, hoping for a scrap of bread, Philip would roar like a walrus till the gull fled. We had just finished playing a doubleheader in a men's summer softball league. The rest of the team had gone home for showers, but we'd headed straight to the deli, as always. He'd ordered a ham sandwich, I believe, to reward me for having hit my first home run of the season. Even though, as he pointed out immediately after I'd reached the dugout, it was an inside-the-park homer and therefore not a REAL homer, like the kind he hit.

"Yonkers?"

"Wedge." I didn't know if his information was correct, but Philip had taught me the regional names for hero sandwiches and my job was to learn them as he instructed, not to challenge his data.

Names, I'd come to understand, mattered when discussing food. It was essential to know what you were talking about, even if correct names were as fluid as the rules that governed my family's diet. Maybe that's why our chatter was as packed with *don'ts* as a hero/hoagie/grinder/sub/wedge was with fillings.

"Very good. Don't put the napkin on the seat." *How did he know I'd just wiped my lips?*

"I'm done with my cream soda," he said. "Let me have a sip of yours."

I was, thanks in large part to Philip, a serious student of food information. Not a scholar, not in my brother's league at all, but no slouch either. Even after our father's market was sold and he went to work in the garment district, even after he died, we felt it was our business to recognize fine culinary distinctions, particularly among meats and fish. To carry on the tradition. By the time Philip left home to marry, when I was sixteen, I could differentiate between littleneck and cherrystone clams by taste alone, and knew that soft-shell clams really had hard shells and were best for steaming. I knew that head cheese was not cheese, but jellied meat from a cow's head, and that the baloney with pearly white chunks of fat scattered throughout was called Mortadella, which—since I'd taken Latin in school—sounded to me like Death Meat. I knew, of course, that the difference between a capon and a pullet had more to do with tenderness than gender. I knew that gefilte fish was made from pike or carp, which was like a Jewish version of scrapple, which was a Pennsylvania Dutch con-coction made of boiled pig scraps and cornmeal. The connection, Philip had explained, was that both were garbage foods given fancy names to make them sound better.

Our teacher-student relationship regarding food was like our coach-rookie relationship regarding softball, where Philip was the team's founder, captain, and slugger, and I was the fourteen-year-old shortstop among men in their twenties, a slick fielder and a speedy singles hitter, learning the game. But as I sat there beside him, chewing and acing his quiz, I knew in my rebellious adolescent soul that the secret to a hero sandwich was the bread. Had to be crusty outside and chewy-soft inside. Philip said I was a fool, it was all about the proper mass and balance of ingredients. Which was why the plain ham sandwich we were eating did not hold up to a hero's standards.

As a high school football and baseball player, I somehow remained lean despite my family's eating habits. Maybe it was all the exercise I got, or youthful metabolism, or the fact that I had distractions that sometimes made me rush away from the table. Maybe, as I often hoped, not being fat meant I was not really my parents' child. My mother, barely five feet tall, weighed 180 pounds. My father, in the years shortly before his death, was all belly and jowl, a man only three inches taller than his very short wife and at least as heavy. My brother, the only one of us to grow taller than five-four, eventually topped out at five-nine and 350 pounds. Through college and into the early years of my first marriage, I held my weight at 150. But then, at the age of twenty-five, I lost control. At my peak, I carried 200 pounds spread over my sixty-four-inch frame.

I still tried to play ball with my friends, but my knees and back hurt from carrying all those pounds. I wore soft, wide shoes to cushion the load, and spent my weekends in an vast ochre jumpsuit. I met people who hadn't seen me in a couple of years and barely recognized me. At a Skloot family picnic during the summer of 1974, a cousin joked that I was finally starting to look like a member of my family. One evening, dressed in undershorts and walking past a mirror in my den, I glanced sideways and saw that I was already shaped like my father in his final years. All I needed to complete the look was a fat Havana cigar.

Late that fall, I invented a diet that I thought I could manage. First, I focused on breakfasts, changing my morning habits but not worrying about lunches or dinners yet. No more breakfasts in restaurants. No sausage and gravy, ham and eggs with an extra order of ham, hash browns, buttered toast, side of pancakes. I ate a bowl of cereal at home, with my infant daughter beside me in her high chair sharing the same meal, both of us playing with our Cheerios and jabbering at each other. At work, when colleagues went out for mid-morning coffee and snacks, I forced myself to stay at my desk. For a month, that was all I did about dieting. Then, when I felt in control of my morning eating, I worked on lunch. No more lunches in restaurants, I told myself, till I weighed 150 pounds again. No ham. I brought to work baggies filled with sliced carrot sticks and celery stalks, red pepper strips, rounds of cucumber, cherry tomatoes, apple slices. For protein, I brought a small chunk of low-fat cheese or a few almonds. At lunch time, I retreated to a disused vault in the state capitol building where I worked, and ate as I read the daily newspaper. Before long, and without saying anything about it, two friends began to join me. I hadn't realized they'd noticed what I was doing. Craig and Ruby said they wanted to lose weight too, but I believe they were actually trying to support me. Instead of going to the newsstand at mid-afternoon and buying a candy bar from the vendor there, I went for a quick walk with Craig and Ruby up the capitol's five flights of stairs. By early February, with my morning and afternoon eating mastered, I worked on dinner and evening snacks. Small portions of chicken or fish. Salad, green vegetables, no ham.

There is a photograph of me, taken just before my diet began, wearing a white tee shirt and bulging with fat all around my daughter's small form as she sleeps in my arms. A companion photograph, taken during our trip to Disney World in March 1975, shows me in a pair of new shorts and a vertically striped polo shirt, fifty-two pounds lighter, seated beside her in a toy car into which I'd never have been able to fit five months earlier. Nearby, oddly enough, was a Disney World staffer dressed as Porky Pig. Ham incarnate.

It was late September 1984, the night before my second marathon, and I was carbo-loading with a group of fellow runners at an Italian restaurant in Portland. The atmosphere was business-like, a half dozen skinny men and women too busy fueling themselves to joke around, argue, or brag about their best times. In lieu of chatter, silverware clanked. Huge bowls of pasta circled the table, followed by bread and a small plate of skinless, boneless, grilled chicken breast. We all ate at least two helpings. But if I weren't eating to fuel a twenty-six mile run, I'd have had less than half a serving.

Once I began long-distance running, in 1982, I also began evaluating my weight by the ounce. Childhood's dietary rules may have been complex, the parsing of minute distinctions among poultry or types of baloney fanatical, my history with food bizarre, but my midlife weight management techniques verged on the pathological. I kept records of miles run and food consumed. Though I normally ran close to fifty miles a week, I would add more miles to compensate for the occasional large meals that accompanied social occasions. But I weighed less at age thirty-seven than I'd weighed in junior high school, I talked and worried about my weight all the time. Diagnosed with high cholesterol despite the good diet and exercise, I took medication and became even more rigorous about what I ate. If I liked it, I avoided it, or found substitutes that would have made my brother weep, buying ham and baloney made out of isolated soy protein and wheat gluten, yolkless egg substance sold in milk cartons, cereals and cookies that were both sugar-free and taste-free.

I thought I had my diet under control. I thought I had broken all my childhood food habits and escaped the family's culinary grip. But the truth was that food was still the center of attention.

After becoming disabled in 1988, I couldn't run, couldn't exercise, and was often bed-bound. So I dreaded adding weight. For a few years after getting sick, I was as crazy in my restricted eating as I'd been when running. If the first half of my life was about obsessive excess around food, the second half threatened to be about obsessive diligence.

Gradually, I came to understand that I needed to ease my grip, that the stress I felt over diet and weight was making my other health problems worse. I needed to integrate everything I did into an overall strategy of consistent health management. I had to rest for several hours daily, lower my expectations about what I could accomplish, structure a life that was stable and balanced. Illness, it turned out, eventually nudged eating from the center of my attention. It was, after all, acceptable to eat what I wanted. I'd even grown to like soy baloney and soy cheese, cereals sweetened with fruit juice, cooked vegetables, raw nuts. I no longer wanted the food of my childhood, so it was no longer necessary to untangle the rules that governed it.

Except for ham. I still have dreams about ham sandwiches. In last night's, for instance, I was wandering through an unknown city feeling hopelessly lost and disoriented. Then I noticed a pushcart in the distance, where a man was selling baguettes so stuffed with ham that they seemed impossible to eat. Sandwiches were stacked behind the cart's glassed front and drooped from its edges. More sandwiches dangled from the cart's roof like skewered fowl in a butcher shop while others peeped like flowers from wicker baskets on the ground. I approached the cart and realized that suddenly I felt at home, though I still didn't know where I was. I reached out, the vendor said, "Don't get any on the seat," and I awoke just before touching the proffered sandwich.

I knew right away what the dream reflected: my walks to our apartment after teaching classes at the Paris Writers Workshop.

At the boulangerie where I bought my sandwiches, the counter display was like the pushcart's in my dream, baguettes everywhere, cut and laid open, their centers stuffed with meats that stained the wax paper wrapping, and though I couldn't read the signs I had no trouble deciphering the choices. It felt as though Philip were hovering over my shoulder, urging me to buy one that had the greatest variety of meats. But I chose the plain ham sandwich with lots of lettuce, *jambon et salade*, then walked happily—even jauntily— down the Rue de Sèvres, eating amidst a shower of crumbs, feeling almost purely at home.

Surely this feeling wasn't associated with ham alone, with satisfying my hunger in a way that was so deeply rooted. I think it was associated with freedom, with a sense of Home as the place where I could enact my deepest desires because they were truly mine, not my brother's or mother's or father's. They were right for me, trust-worthy. I could allow myself to eat and enjoy, guilt-free, a *jambon et salade* sandwich knowing it was something I could do in moderation. Besides, after so many years of slow neurological recovery, I was now capable of walking off the calories. The feeling of being at home was present, too, because Philip was there, alive within me eight years after he had died from complications of diabetes brought on by morbid obesity. He was yakking as usual about my choices. I listened to him, but I could make my own decision. And the bread in my dream, like the baguette in Paris, was perfect, crusty on the outside but chewy-soft inside.

16

Flesh and Fortune:

Coming Back to *Measure for Measure*

I'm sitting in the campus cafeteria eating lunch with Gary Blackton, professor of management at Concordia University in Portland, Oregon. My ham sandwich refuses to hold together no matter how many times I rearrange its elements. Despite Gary's laryngitis and the raucous chatter of students all around us, despite having heard him speak only once in the last forty years, his baritone voice is so familiar to me that it triggers a rush of memories. He's silent now, eating his split pea soup, but I keep hearing him cry out "Death is a fearful thing."

I know Gary not as Professor Blackton but as Claudio, the condemned romantic hero of Shakespeare's *Measure for Measure*, from a 1967 production we acted in together as students at Franklin and Marshall College. While he played the heartthrob, his thirty-five speeches filled with poetry and memorable lines that showed great depths of soul, I played Pompey the pimp and bartender, a typical Shakespearean clown or fool, whose sixty speeches contained exactly two lines of poetry that showed his sense of self-inflation.

The part of Claudio seemed to fit Gary well; for me, portraying Pompey let me become something altogether alien. But I loved being the bawdy jester, becoming someone wise to the ways of the world, especially the ways of men and women together, trusting his own instincts, listening to the counsel of city officials but determined to make his way "as the flesh and fortune shall better determine."

Gary and I weren't close friends back then, didn't socialize outside The Green Room Theater or have classes together, but every night for two months we rehearsed the play, doing scenes over and over, the whole cast coming to know one another's voices intimately. I remember Gary sitting in the back of the empty theater, legs draped over the seat in front of him, reading and reading act 3, scene 1, trying to pace his long speech about the thoughts howling through his brain as he contemplates imminent death. "Ay, but to die, and go we know not where . . . ." I remember him walking around backstage muttering as he practiced the tongue-twisting lines: "To bathe in fiery floods or to reside / In thrilling region of thick-ribbèd ice." I remember his slender, sleek grace onstage, the strange distance he projected as Claudio, agitated by a deep sadness for his Juliet, pregnant before marriage and destined to raise his child alone.

Until three years ago, I hadn't seen Gary Blackton since the autumn night that production closed. But then he showed up in the audience for a 2004 reading I gave in Portland. I didn't recognize his face. Afterward, when he said "Hi Floyd," I knew who he was before he said his name.

Now in the cafeteria, when Gary speaks of his love for teaching, his passion for the art of management, his theory of strategic triangulation, I continue to lose track of the words, seeing him instead fallen on his knees, hands clasped across his chest, begging his cloistered sister, the "fair maid" Isabella, to spare his life by agreeing to yield her virginity to the Duke's "outward-sainted deputy," Angelo: "What sin you do to save a brother's life / Nature dispenses with the deed so far / That it becomes a virtue."

First performed in 1604, roughly the same period as *Othello*, *All's Well That Ends Well*, *King Lear*, and *Macbeth*, *Measure for Measure* isn't as frequently staged or written about as Shakespeare's more famous plays. But it's one that grabs hold of you.

Harold Bloom, in *Shakespeare: The Invention of the Human*, calls *Measure for Measure* "the masterpiece of nihilism" and marvels at its "essential wildness," its "high rancidity," saying "no other work by Shakespeare is so fundamentally alienated from the Western synthesis of Christian morality and Classical ethics." The play seems to terrify him, calling forth descriptions such as "mad," "insane," "sadistic," and "outrageous." Rattled, Bloom finds that it "harbors a deeper distrust of nature, reason, society, and revelation than the ensuing tragedies manifest." Along with *Macbeth*, it's his favorite Shakespeare.

In *Shakespeare After All*, Marjorie Garber takes special note of the play's "dramatic patterns and psychological investigations," which make this so-called comedy "fit superbly well" with "its chronological neighbors among the tragedies." Frank Kermode, in *Shakespeare's Language*, admires "the relative power of the verse" and finds that the play, "for about half its length, is one of the truly great plays." Barbara Everett, in an essay published by the *London Review of Books*, says the play "startles us, it is outre, it goes too far—but it also has a marvellousness wholly its own, original." Clearly, this is a memorably disturbing work.

Measure for Measure is set in a hothouse Vienna where sexual liberty appears to be weakening the community's moral stability. The convoluted plot relies heavily on disguise, confusion, misdirection. The Duke, witnessing the licentious behavior of his people, blames himself for failing to uphold laws he promulgated to govern their conduct. "Our decrees, / Dead to infliction, to themselves are dead." He decides to leave town for a while and appoints the righteous Deputy Duke, Angelo, "a man of stricture and firm abstinence," to take his place and improve matters: "Your scope is as mine own, / So to enforce or qualify the laws / As to your soul seems good."

The cold, harsh Angelo, "a man whose blood / Is snow-broth," cracks down on vice, both in general, by closing the brothels, and in specific, by arresting Claudio for having gotten his fiancée pregnant. He is sentenced to hang. When Claudio's sister, a novice in the Order of Saint Clare, shows up to beg for her brother's life, Angelo finds himself so overwhelmed by desire that his rectitude vanishes and he offers to spare Claudio if Isabella will sleep with him. "This virtuous maid / Subdues me quite."

The working-out of this dilemma occurs against a backdrop of Vienna's thriving erotic life, its various clandestine romances, flagrant prostitution trade, and general debauchery. In many ways, the fast-talking Pompey, who operates a suburban tavern/whorehouse for the aging Mistress Overdone, is the mouthpiece of this world. As critic Marjorie Garber notes, "He speaks more wisdom than he knows." He understands that people will follow their sexual urges despite the government's policies, and pointedly asks the city's primary Judge, Escalus, "Does your worship mean to geld and splay all the youth of the city?" Ignored, seeing that Angelo intends to clamp down on the carnal underworld, Pompey adds some parting advice for the judge about a policy of capital punishment for fornicators: "If you head and hang all that offend that way but for ten year together, you'll be glad to give out a commission for more heads."

The Duke, disguised as a monk, returns to witness Angelo's behavior as well as the high and low shenanigans of his citizenry, interceding at last to turn this near-tragedy into a comedy by arranging for some very unlikely but traditional resolutions in which everyone's life is spared and an octet of unsuitable characters marry one another.

If *Measure for Measure* were submitted as a writing workshop assignment, you might be tempted to tell the playwright, "Good job, but it needs a little more work." The play can be seen as a rambling, baggy, sloppily plotted work, full of improbabilities, with flaws in its time scheme and scenes that contradict other scenes. As the action progresses, characters come in and out of focus, or fullness, and the play ends as vaguely, as unconvincingly, as it began. For example, at times we're told that the Duke leaves Vienna in order to let someone else enforce the laws he has overlooked, but at other times the reason is to test Angelo's character. These are mutually exclusive intentions, since the Duke's knowledge of and doubts about Angelo's character, the very things he wants to test, make him an unsuitable substitute. Another drawback of the play's construction is that the Duke continually explains what he plans to do, then does it, as though Shakespeare weren't sure we could follow the plot's intricacies or the Duke's motivations otherwise. Or that they would seem too far-fetched without this added effort at rationale, as when the Duke himself becomes a kind of pimp, convincing Isabella to agree to Angelo's demands, but then substituting Angelo's jilted fiancée, Mariana—disguised as Isabella—as the bed partner.

But altogether it is filled with such power and richness of situation, uses such intricately developed linguistic resonances, and generates such intensity among its leading characters, that tinkering with its flaws would seem beside the point. The play transcends the apparent limitations of its design and faults in construction.

I've reread *Measure for Measure* twice in the last year, and find myself thinking more and more about the play, about the way it has changed for me over time. Now, reading it in the final two years of the George W. Bush administration, I'm compelled by its portrayal of political leaders who don't understand themselves or their people, of lawmakers and judges who fail to appreciate the human dimension or the spirit of laws they seek to uphold. The play features public figures who rely on rhetoric rather than truthful speech, though "truth is truth / To th' end of reck'ning," and this wreaks genuine havoc among the citizenry. I see in *Measure for Measure* a state that routinely spies on its citizens and interferes with their private lives, that attempts to regulate intimate behavior even while its leaders commit the very crimes they seek to condemn. The play moves me, and leaves me longing to hear my own political leaders recognize what the Duke recognizes at the play's end, after boldly facing up to his administration's failures: "I have seen corruption boil and bubble / Till it o'errun the stew." He does something about it, too, even if what he does defies credibility, and his impulse toward corrective action gives the play its essentially positive spin.

Normally, I wouldn't have noticed such issues, since my way of reading naturally gravitates toward the characters' personal emotional stories rather than the larger political dimension. But we live in strange times, times that make the political intensely personal, and I was surprised by the play's contemporary relevance. Why, the Duke even cloaks himself in the trappings and language of religion— a monk's robes, speeches rich in biblical allusion—and the Deputy Duke quotes the highest of ideals, to conduct their activities.

Equally compelling is the play's portrayal of its characters' internal struggles. *Measure for Measure* is relentless in probing the effort to live with integrity, as characters are forced to recognize what can't be denied in themselves and act accordingly. All the play's major figures face the contradiction between their ideals and their behaviors: Angelo, who can't suppress his passion for Isabella despite his fulminations against unrestrained passion; Claudio, who doesn't want to taint his sister's honor but, fearing death, begs her to yield to Angelo; the Duke, who wants to escape from the mess his lax leadership has created but must return to right the ship of state himself; Isabella, who yearns to live compassionately, to sacrifice herself for God, but can't bring herself to move beyond her ideals for the sake of her brother's life.

Older, almost but not quite as wise now as I pretended to be at twenty, when playing Pompey, I was struck by a related theme when rereading the play: the notion of shedding disguises, as the Duke must do, uncloaking himself, no longer keeping his distance, getting his hands dirtied in the mess of human desires. As Angelo must do, when confronted in public with his hypocrisy. "O, what may man within him hide, / Though angel on the outward side!" *Measure for Measure* is a play of revelations, both self-revelations and public revelations, in which understanding the importance of what's hidden proves to be the essential lesson for everyone. Motives and secret behaviors come to light, and this process is meant to be restorative of shattered lives and shattered community, meant to lead everyone on the path of forgiveness because "the best men are molded out of faults."

Having acted in *Measure for Measure* in 1967, playing my first role in serious theater, I took the play in deeply then. Counting the reading I did prior to auditioning, the cast read-through prior to the beginning of rehearsals, the two months of scene-by-scene work, the run-throughs as opening night neared, three dress rehearsals, and eight performances, I probably "read" *Measure for Measure* at least twenty times that year.

For me at that time, the play was simply and fully about sex. In scene after scene, I saw the force of desire at work, "the wanton stings and motions of the sense." I believed completely that Angelo was undone by being near Isabella, by engaging with her mind, by hearing her argue and oppose him, by her purity. Those scenes to me were electric with carnality, even before the actors found their chemistry together. I saw desire override all the high ideals espoused by the characters. Virtue, faith, mercy, law, wisdom lost all power, revealed as nothing more than words that slip from the tongue when passion and desire take hold. *Measure for Measure* was about the ways of men and women together—honest, worldly, earthy. "It is impossible to extirp it quite," a character says of sexual expression, "till eating and drinking be put down." I agreed. Most of the play's good lines were about sex. Even the ones that weren't directly about sex or relationships between men and women were about sex or relationships between men and women for me: "Alack, when once our grace we have forgot, / Nothing goes right." Everything else that occurred in the play was tangential, as I read it.

In Pompey's very first speeches, he talks about Claudio's arrest, and his tone is knowing, witty, experienced. Asked what the prisoner has done, Pompey replies, "a woman," and he describes the particular offense as "groping for trouts in a peculiar river," a line whose meaning gave me endless delight once I learned that "groping for trouts" referred to a method of catching them by stroking their gills, and that "peculiar" meant private. Pompey also announces the news that all suburban houses of prostitution will be torn down, and all urban brothels left to "stand for seed." So in his initial appearance, he brings news of both private and public sexual significance. I saw him as vastly experienced in the ways of erotic life, something I myself was not. But for two hours each night during the play's run, I knew what was what. I had been around, and could be lucid, from the inside, about sexual life, about a world gone wild with deceit and hypocrisy over desire. I could be so experienced in these matters that I found the playful side of erotic life.

For over a year, I'd considered auditioning for a play in The Green Room. As a sophomore, having declared myself an English major, I started going to the college theater's productions, admiring *Twelfth Night*, *Julius Caesar*, *The Caucasian Chalk Circle*, *The Streets of New York*. I recognized and anticipated the various actors' strengths, and felt a growing interest in performing again. Besides, since Franklin and Marshall was then all-male, being in the theater was a handy way to meet women—faculty family members, department secretaries, volunteers from within the local community—who might be in the cast.

Through my early teen years, I'd been dragged along by my mother to appear with her in community theater productions, playing one of the chorus of kids in *The King and I*, or a smart-aleck adolescent in *Auntie Mame*. And I'd played A-rab in that summer camp performance of *West Side Story* at fifteen, spurred on by the chance to spend rehearsal time with girls from our sister-camp.

But I'd stopped after that, refusing to take part in my mother's theater world anymore, turning instead to baseball, football, and basketball. After hurting my shoulder and being forced to stop playing baseball, I was involved in no extracurricular activities. So when tryouts for *Measure for Measure* were announced, early in my junior year, I signed up. It was time to find out if I liked acting as much as I thought I might, freed of my mother's presence, and it was time to find something other than sports as a means of expression.

What I found, besides friendships and camaraderie, was an introduction to craft. There was Gary Blackton, night after night, sitting in the back of the theater working out the rush of his character's frightened imaginings. There was John Ogden, the actor playing Constable Elbow, on stage for only two scenes in the play but remaining throughout rehearsal to help other cast members practice lines and to suggest alternative readings. Lou Hampton, who played the leading role—the Duke—and would become my roommate and closest friend, had learned all 194 of his character's speeches before many of us had committed our much smaller roles to heart. As we walked to the tavern after rehearsals, he would speak in character, sometimes even in rhyming couplets, describing the autumn weather or the classwork he had to finish before morning. Acting, it turned out, could be approached in ways other than my mother's, which was the only way I'd known. It could involve more than simply memorizing your lines, or approximating them as she had done, and then reciting them while blinking your eyes a lot. It could involve emotional engagement, intense preparation. The actor playing

Angelo, Fred Hoff, who would also become a roommate, seemed to find endless ways to inflect the word "Fie!" He could make it convey fury, self-loathing, surprise, disdain. He could make it fill the theater or disappear like a stifled cry.

I found acting, as I eventually found writing, could lead you into dark corners, secret places, and require that you bring them to light, give them voice and form. Late in *Measure for Measure*, the capricious and loudmouth character Lucio, Claudio's close friend, has a speech that made a deep impression on me. Lamenting Claudio's imminent death, moved by Isabella's sorrow, fearing for his own life because he too has made a woman pregnant out of wedlock, and frustrated by the absence of the state's leader, Lucio blurts out, "If the old fantastical duke of dark corners had been at home, he [Claudio] had lived." Lucio calls him the *duke of dark corners* because of his secretive machinations and devious use of disguises and surveillance, tactics with which he clearly has a history. Unknown to Lucio, but clear to the audience, the Duke in his Monk's garb has access to various characters' inner, secret lives, to their dark corners. He takes confessions, asks probing questions, and manipulates behavior in ways that would be impossible—even for the Duke—without the religious trappings. These dark corners, where characters reveal their deepest truths, not only allow the plot to resolve, they open the human heart to our scrutiny. Lighting the dark corners was Shakespeare's great gift as a playwright, and is the source of his plays' endurance.

Even as Pompey, I had scenes that could only work if I found the dark corners from which his words emerged. Though typically a clever wiseguy who prefers the quick answer and verbal joust to the serious revelation, Pompey has a moment of genuinely soulful openness in his final long appearance onstage. Imprisoned, his livelihood outlawed and place of business torn down, finding himself without advocate or source of appeal, no one on whom to work his double-talking antics, Pompey comes out on stage alone at the start

222—TRAVELS IN LAVENDER AND LIGHT

of act 4, scene 3. He has, in the previous scene, agreed to become the prison's assistant executioner, a career change brought on by necessity and something resembling acceptance: "I have been an unlawful bawd time out of mind, but yet I will be content to be a lawful hangman." Now, having the run of the prison, he enters a room that he finds filled with familiar faces. "One would think it were Mistress Overdone's own house, for here be many of her old customers." He proceeds to name them and the crimes that landed them here. It was a difficult speech to memorize because it lacked any logical development or poetic rhythm, was just names and crimes. But it felt crucial to the portrayal of this man's central quality: resilience. In trying to find my way through this speech, I found Pompey's dark corner, the lonely and threatening place where resilience was most needed. It is resilience, and the flexibility that makes resilience function, that enables Pompey to be a survivor. It also provides the one moment of poetry in his otherwise prosaic speeches, a rhyming pentameter couplet he utters when threatened with a whipping unless he stops pimping: "Whip me? No, no, let carman whip his jade. / The valiant heart's not whipped out of his trade."

Though I did well enough as Pompey, it took me less than two years to find that my limitations as an actor were too great to overcome. I couldn't achieve what I wanted to achieve, couldn't use acting to satisfy my emerging artistic desires. It became clear that I would be cast again and again as a clown, not as a romantic hero, not as a noble or tragic leader, not even as a complex and compelling villain. I played a file clerk in a courtroom drama, a character present essentially for comic relief. I played a silly French general in an antiwar farce, and a quack doctor in a Restoration comedy. When Sean O'Casey's *Cock-a-Doodle Dandy* was cast, I played the title character, a dancing rooster who represents the drama's life force. My only speeches were blared cock-crowings. In an evening of scenes from various Shakespeare plays, I played four different clowns, all utterly similar to Pompey in *Measure for Measure*: Moth in *Love's Labour's Lost*, the Fool in *King Lear*, Feste in *Twelfth Night*, and the Gravedigger in *Hamlet*. What I brought to the stage, apparently, was a youthful energy, even when playing an old man with a moustache I grew for the role and grayed each night in the dressing room. I conveyed a pint-size lightness of spirit, a mouthiness, and a way of projecting physical comedy in my movements, all of which was so frustrating because I saw myself as serious, as full of gravitas.

My limitations as an actor led directly to finding myself as a writer, where I could either be myself, unadorned, or create characters of my own to inhabit. I think that my experience on stage may have helped sharpen a sense of scene, an understanding of the way voice and dialogue could carry action and define character. It may have helped me grasp the need for flexibility and resilience, for finding new paths when old ones became closed off, as acting itself had. I learned on stage to follow, "as the flesh and fortune shall better determine," my way toward the powerful, urgent zone of dark corners, and seeing what happened if I stayed there long enough.

Gary Blackton says he doesn't remember much about our production of *Measure for Measure*. It's a blur, he says. He has now finished eating his soup and nibbling on his roll, and though I'm still hungry I can't imagine trying to deal with the tatters of my sandwich.

We are talking about The Green Room Theater company, which over the years has produced such accomplished actors as Roy Scheider and Treat Williams, and industry notables such as Franklin Shaffner and James Lapine. We feel proud to have been part of it.

"In central Pennsylvania," Gary says, "it was THE theater. People came to see the plays. They read the reviews and they bought their tickets."

"I remember waiting up for the first review after opening night."

He laughs. "Yeah, till two in the morning." Then he stops and looks at me intensely for a moment. "What I do remember is you as a rooster. Man, you had so much energy. That's what the play was about, the Irish Church's defeat of life-energy. And there you were, crouched in a corner, then jumping all around the stage, running on the walls, flapping your wings. You became the rooster, all right."

I'm not sure he realizes how little pride this makes me feel. But I love hearing him talk anyway. And I remember another of his speeches as Claudio, can hear it like a voiceover as we sit and smile at each other:

"Our natures do pursue, / Like rats that raven down their proper bane, / A thirsty evil, and when we drink, we die." This speech about human desire and a state that punishes its expression is among the darkest in the play. It expresses the character's feeling of entrapment when his decent, basic nature comes crosswise of the law. As the plot resolves, though, Claudio doesn't die, and following his nature is eventually seen as acceptable.

In all my rereadings of *Measure for Measure*, I've heard this pivotal speech spoken in Gary's voice, as though my earliest experience of the play had, in fact, never fully faded despite the later, deeper understanding of its messages. And come to appreciate what it meant for me as an acting experience, all those years ago, a pathway into my own future work.

Gary and I rise to return our trays. We hug, and I head out into the spring sunlight.

Epilogue
Silence the Pianos

A year ago today, my mother stopped eating. She was ninety-six, and could no longer walk or use the toilet without help. She'd stopped talking, stopped humming, no longer smiled or showed signs of contact with the world. There seemed little that approximated consciousness anymore.

I knew it was a mercy that her body had begun its final retreat. Beverly and I spent time with my mother then. We sat by her bed and talked to her or sang her favorite songs, trying to ease her way. Eyes closed, breath shallow, lips sealed, she lay on her side and faced the wall. She didn't seem to hear us. Light fell across her body and flickered as a spring wind passed through leaves outside her open window.

Just before Beverly and I left, I moved my mother's bed out far enough to squeeze myself between it and the wall so that she might feel my breath as the last song ended. Suddenly her eyes opened wide. They moved across the space between us, across my face, then shut. I felt sure that nothing had registered in her mind, but was glad for the last glimpse we shared. I knew then it was time for silence.

It's a Sunday in the mid-1950s, and my father, brother, and I wait in the tiny foyer of our Brooklyn apartment. We're going out to dinner at Lundy's in Sheepshead Bay. Dressed in winter coats, mufflers, and gloves, wreathed in my father's cigar smoke, we can hear my mother moving around in her bedroom. She's trying to decide what jewelry to wear, or changing shoes, or touching up her lipstick. "That woman," my father grumbles, "would be late to her own funeral."

And fifty years later, she was. I'm still not sure how that happened. Long before her death, I'd made all the arrangements for transporting her body from Oregon to New York, for its care in New York, and for its arrival at the family plot on Long Island. "Planning for tomorrow today," the funeral home literature urged. I had.

Everything was going according to that plan as Beverly and I flew east a day before the funeral. But when we landed, there were several frantic messages on our cell phone. The cemetery staff wouldn't dig my mother's grave unless I gave them permission to move a small shrub that had grown near its edge. We got that taken care of, confirmed that her body was where it needed to be, and were all set for her funeral the next morning at 10:00.

Beverly and I, along with my daughter Rebecca and her boyfriend David, left their Jersey City apartment in time to arrive at the cemetery fifteen minutes early. My childhood friend Larry Salander was already there, sitting in his car near the gravesite, the air conditioning turned up. My stepbrother and his family were there as well, son of the man my mother had married in 1966. The rabbi I'd hired by phone, sight-unseen, was there too, talking about his life-affirming experience a few years earlier, when he gave blessings to the Philadelphia Phillies baseball team during their spring training on the west coast of Florida. The grave had been dug and the gravediggers rested under a nearby tree, waiting for the second installment of their work to begin. But my mother's body hadn't arrived.

We all gathered by the door of the cemetery's office, as my father and brother and I had always gathered by the apartment door, and talked in whispers. The hearse finally pulled through the main gates at 10:20, headlights shining, morning sunlight gleaming off the bumpers. Rebecca looked at me and broke into a huge smile: her grandmother had managed one final grand entrance.

The nine mourners walked together back to the gravesite. Over the years, the Skloot family plot had nearly filled, my father's parents in the center of the back row, underneath the obelisk that bore our name, his siblings and their spouses arrayed around them. In the plot's far left corner, space had been left for my mother to rest between my father and step-father, whose presence there was the result of her two-decades-long campaign. She'd been absolutely determined to lie between her husbands, despite the wishes of either family.

I was prepared to see her gravesite, the gaping hole, the mounded dirt. But not to see that my father's gravestone had been removed from its place and turned backward, as though indicating that he couldn't bear to witness her arrival. Nor to see that my stepfather's grave and stone had been covered completely in the dirt removed to accommodate my mother. Metaphors everywhere!

Rebecca and I had fashioned, separately, our simple tributes. I spoke about my mother's flamboyance and talents, her love of song, her transformation over the last few years. I read a poem about cycles of time. Rebecca, with typical grace and insight, handed out the lyrics to a song she remembered my mother singing to her in childhood. Her lovely alto led us through the four stanzas of Manos Hadjidakis's 1960 tune, "Never On Sunday," with its flirtatious fun and high spirits, its simultaneous embrace of and rigorous limits on the expression of love.

The aptness of Rebecca's choice made me think of other great funeral orations: Marc Antony's speech over his friend's body in *Julius Caesar*, Nehru's eulogy for Mohandas Ghandi, Robert F. Kennedy's for Martin Luther King Jr. Her memorial for her grandmother did what the best of them do, capturing something of their subject's essence, conveying love and loss and, sometimes, a sense of reconciliation. And she did it without the high rhetoric that often accompanies eulogies, a rhetoric that would have been wrong for the occasion. She got right to the heart of things. She used a song. She made us laugh.

In the 1994 film *Four Weddings and a Funeral*, actor John Hannah plays a character named Matthew, who recites the W. H. Auden poem "Funeral Blues" at the service in honor of his dear friend Gareth. That poem, never one of Auden's most well known, has become a kind of griever's touchstone now:

> Stop all the clocks, cut off the telephone,
> Prevent the dog from barking with a juicy bone,
> Silence the pianos and with muffled drum
> Bring out the coffin, let the mourners come.

When I reread the poem a few days after the funeral, the phrase *silence the pianos* triggered sudden tears that shocked me. I was sure that my mother's long decline and my years of preparation for it, the comfort of being with my wife and daughter, the graveside songs and laughter, had left me more settled about her death. But I found myself imagining my mother in her heyday, seated at the piano and banging out one of her signature songs, Gershwin or Rodgers and Hart, her stout body rising off the bench, her eyes closing as she leaned way over to the right, straining to reach the notes for her grand finale. I realized that her music had been playing in my head, off and on, for days. And it felt as though little could have brought home more clearly what had happened to her over time than the silencing of the pianos.

I've always maintained that I don't believe in the afterlife. Heavenly paradise, hosts of angels with their harps, reunions with loved ones. None of the traditional images or comforts makes much sense to me. I don't believe in lingering spirits, the souls of the departed sending messages back from the other side. I don't believe in reincarnation.

In part, all this may be because my Jewish religious background, unlike Islam or Christianity, never emphasized the afterlife. The idea, as Rabbi Joseph Telushkin says in his book, *Jewish Literacy*, "is rarely discussed in Jewish life." The Torah, Judaism's central text, "makes no clear reference to the afterlife at all." As my friend Julia Neuberger, a British rabbi, says in her book, *On Being Jewish*, "Jews are what Christians might call 'a bit shaky' on the afterlife." It's not that Jewish thought rejects the possibility of life after death, just that it's vague about the details. There's a general notion of eventual resurrection of the dead in messianic times, a world-to-come that's never given specific form. As a child, nothing crystalized for me on the subject, and as an adult, nothing compelled me to overcome my doubts. In the forty-six years since his death, I have never felt the presence of my father. Nor of my brother, dead since 1997. They are gone, as my mother now is gone, from this or any other world.

Yet I sure do write a lot about the afterlife. I've written poems imagining my brother getting to win all he wants in a hereafter casino, or coming back to reveal himself in the landscape around me. I've written of my father standing at the finish line of a race I'm running, anticipating the moment he can escort me across and into the mist beyond. As my mother's health declined, I wrote several poems in which my father awaited her arrival in the next world, one in which they began their mutual torment all over again. I've written about William Butler Yeats finding himself among the ghosts with whom he always longed to commune, and wanting nothing more than to return to life. I've written about Rasputin returning to the world; Gauguin dead and adrift in the afterlife, still yearning for paradise; Brooklyn Dodgers shortstop Pee Wee Reese coming out of evening shadows on the anniversary of his death to teach me something about the here and now; T. S. Eliot wandering the hillside where Beverly and I lived, overseeing our quest for water after the well had run dry.

For all my rational belief, I understand that my poems say something different. By remembering the dead as I do, by keeping them in my mind and heart and life, by writing about them, I'm keeping them alive in my world—my inner world—and defying my own carefully wrought Position on the Afterlife.

Clearly, I still have work to do in bringing my deepest feelings and statements of belief into harmony. Writing is what reveals this to me. I see that I'm not drawn to articulating ideology or philosophy, that I concentrate instead on the emotional and sensory elements of my experience. That the forming of abstract ideas isn't fundamental to my creative process. And when I do form them, pushing against my neurological limitations, when I do try to express certain beliefs, I fail to fully recognize and incorporate those emotional or sensory elements. This is particularly true in the area of spirituality, faith, religious mystery.

Writing about my mother's death, about being the only survivor of my immediate family, has brought this into sharper focus. It has led me to question myself about the afterlife because I can't deny that the topic emerges vividly, over and over, from the place where my writing begins. I see the obvious now, that belief in the afterlife is embedded in a confrontation with death—the loss of loved ones, the prospect of one's own death—and that my situation is hardly unique.

It heartens me to think that my daughter is also a writer, and that the work of remembrance is passing into her capable hands. With a bachelor's degree in biological sciences and master's degree in creative nonfiction writing, she is both trained and inclined to look at the sort of questions I tend to avoid, bringing together feelings and facts and ideas, inner and outer worlds, observation and belief, details and conclusions. Her first book rescues and resurrects a forgotten figure in the history of medical research, Henrietta Lacks, a cancer victim in the 1950s whose virulent, immortal cells have fueled more than half a century of life-saving discoveries. If anything gives form to my emerging sense of an afterlife, it is Rebecca and the work she does.

On a Sunday morning in November, about seven months after my mother's death, Beverly and I returned to the New York gravesite to mark the unveiling of her gravestone. This is a Jewish custom resonant with finality, not only ending the traditional period of mourning but putting in place an enduring monument etched with birth and death dates. I was glad to see that my father's gravestone had been put back in its proper place, and my stepfather's grave restored to its proper shape. It looked like everyone there had accepted her arrival after all.

There was, too, a sense of near-completion to the family plot. All but four of the allocated spaces were filled, with only two aged aunts and two unmarried cousins still surviving, the story of the first generation of American Skloots in its final pages.

I said the mourner's Kaddish. I placed stones beside my parents' graves and beside my stepfather's, marking my presence there, another Jewish custom. For someone who doesn't believe in the afterlife, I sure looked like someone enacting ritual acknowledgments of continuity and sending messages to The Beyond.

As we began to leave the gravesite, I turned back as though summoned, and took a long, hard look. Clock time seemed to stop, but I felt myself in the presence of another kind of time altogether, remembering trips to this place with my father and brother when I was a boy and only my grandparents' graves were there. In the distance, a church bell rang, and its fading sound was like one of my mother's great concluding piano chords. Beverly laced her arm through mine and drew me close, standing with me in silence that followed.